Unified Field Theology

Unified Field Theology

A Journey from Evangelical Fundamentalism
to Faith in What Is

GREGORY W. BROWN

Foreword by Donald E. Pitzer

WIPF *&* STOCK · Eugene, Oregon

UNIFIED FIELD THEOLOGY
A Journey from Evangelical Fundamentalism to Faith in What Is

Copyright © 2018 Gregory W. Brown. All rights reserved. Except for brief quotations in critical publications or reviews, no part of this book may be reproduced in any manner without prior written permission from the publisher. Write: Permissions, Wipf and Stock Publishers, 199 W. 8th Ave., Suite 3, Eugene, OR 97401.

Wipf & Stock
An Imprint of Wipf and Stock Publishers
199 W. 8th Ave., Suite 3
Eugene, OR 97401

www.wipfandstock.com

PAPERBACK ISBN: 978-1-5326-5523-4
HARDCOVER ISBN: 978-1-5326-5524-1
EBOOK ISBN: 978-1-5326-5525-8

Manufactured in the U.S.A.   08/22/18

Unless otherwise noted, scriptures taken from the Holy Bible, New International Version®, NIV®. Copyright © 1973, 1978, 1984, 2011 by Biblica, Inc.™ Used by permission of Zondervan. All rights reserved worldwide. www.zondervan.com The "NIV" and "New International Version" are trademarks registered in the United States Patent and Trademark Office by Biblica, Inc.™

To everyone who ever stood at the bottom of a mountain and then climbed it and all those who ever backed off a cliff trusting rappelling equipment for the first time, especially those whose experiences consisted of life and faith rather than rock and rope.

Contents

Foreword by Donald E. Pitzer | *ix*
Acknowledgments | *xi*

1. I Used to Know It All | 1
2. Introduction | 3
3. Terms: How and Why They Will Be Used or Omitted | 5
4. Trouble with Language | 12
5. Paradox: Problem and Promise | 16
6. Global Paradigm Shift | 20
7. My Own Path | 24
8. Know | 27
9. Twenty-First-Century Worldviews | 29
10. The Narrative Implodes | 32
11. The Dark Side of a Shepherd God | 39
12. Gossamer Chains | 43
13. Good and Evil | 46
14. Blaming Those Hurt by the Church | 49
15. Problem with Teachings on Hell | 51
16. The Problem of Heaven | 55
17. Society, Violence, and Religion | 58
18. Competing Worldviews | 62
19. Christianity Is Not Jesus | 66
20. Twenty-First-Century Knowing | 69
21. Surrender to What Is: I Am | 72
22. I Am: Part Two | 76

23 Creating a Space for Truth | 79
24 If Humanity Continues on Paths of Destruction | 81
25 We Have Our Stories | 84
26 Mystical Experiences | 87
27 Myth | 92
28 Dream about Caring Enough to Act | 95
29 How Do We Live? Problems with Current Models | 97
30 Particle Behavior | 100
31 The Gravity of Nothing | 104
32 Right and Wrong | 107
33 How It All Fits | 112
34 The Cross and Suffering | 119
35 Overwhelmed by Size | 122
36 Humility and Gratitude Affirm Existence | 124
37 "Faith Is the Substance of Things Hoped For" | 126
38 Difficulty with the Label "Christian" | 129
39 Living the Paradox by Climbing Rocks | 131
40 Death | 133
41 Death in Space-Time | 137
42 How Much We Matter | 141
43 Expanding the Parameters of How Humans Matter | 144
44 The End of Consumption | 148
45 The Wormhole | 150
46 Life With and Without Magic | 152
47 Bosons and Discourse | 155
48 The Infinity Problem | 158
49 Centering | 160
50 Reexamining Familiar Texts | 164
51 The Two Trees of Genesis 2:9 | 166
52 Humans and Nature in the Bible | 169
53 Science and the Book of Job | 173
54 Our Most Powerful Myth | 177
55 New Fundamentals | 181

Bibliography | 185

Foreword

Every culture must offer its people the answers to ultimate questions: Where did we come from? Why are we here? Where are we going after we die? The answers to these questions are the essence of religion and philosophy from time immemorial.

True believers in the answers given by their cultural heritage often find comfort, purpose, and hope. Those who do not find these answers altogether satisfying often enter upon a difficult but rewarding journey toward more universal truth. We might agree that everyone deserves to strive for and arrive at an intellectual and emotional/religious/spiritual destination of integrity that squares with facts, reason, and experience. How satisfying the ever-broadening conclusions become defines the quality of life and inter-personal and inter-environmental relationships of the seeker. If successful, this process and its results affect the lives and journey of fellow travelers.

Gregory Brown has wholeheartedly embraced this all-encompassing quest. It has been my privilege to know and philosophize with Greg during much of his seeking and finding. While he was a student in my college history classes, we discovered we were walking adjacent paths from evangelical fundamentalist beginnings. I was a member of his doctoral committee, and we have maintained an active dialogue to the present. I am deeply impressed by the open-mindedness, honesty, and persistence that consistently have characterized Dr. Brown's search for truth and that have come through clearly in this series of essays.

He describes a wrenching and reassuring adventure from his evangelical fundamentalist moorings. His brief, readable essays outline his relentless search into Scripture and theology, history and science to arrive at his groundbreaking *unified field theology*. Unified field theology offers a realm in which the physical universe itself holds awesome, powerful, and all-encompassing qualities that have been associated only with the divinities of religions and mythologies. This theology asserts that the human consciousness of "I am" constitutes the essence of meaningful existence by realizing what matters is that we matter to each other. Brown's UFT worldview implies an almost utopian potential for a "faith in what is" that might neutralize the animosities and violent conflicts still so often characterizing the relationship among and within traditional religions.

Some may find Gregory Brown's new orientation disturbing. Others may find it comforting. Some may find it controversial. Others may find it conciliatory. All will find it thought-provoking. Those who discover his evidence, analysis, and conclusions convincing may also find them transformative.

Donald E. Pitzer
Professor Emeritus of History and Director Emeritus of the Center for Communal Studies of the University of Southern Indiana

Acknowledgments

This book is based on a lifetime of study, experience, questions, and the exploration of possibilities. I owe a great deal to a multitude of teachers—some of them in actual classes, some of them friends and elders, and some of them considered by the system to be my students. The journey would not have been possible without them.

I am especially grateful to three people who served as readers, questioners, and friends as the essays in this book were created and edited: David Melchior, fellow outdoorsman, teacher of children that others label impossible, and lifelong religious skeptic; Don Janzen, retired anthropologist and expert on past and present American communal societies who taught me many things about anthropology and seeing life through the eyes of others through many conversations that never included a formal class; and Don Pitzer, history professor recognized for global leadership in the field of intentional community and developmental communalism, my undergraduate advisor, lifelong mentor, friend, fellow seeker, and spiritual brother. Many times on my journey, Don Pitzer, affectionately known to many as Doc, was the one person with whom I could share new thoughts and questions in the safety of our mutual pursuit of truth and light.

I am grateful to Tim Van Meter, lifelong friend and participant in many long conversations as we both journeyed from a common childhood faith to more complex and informed views of the world. He has often suggested for me the next text suitable for continuing my journey of understanding in the various views of theology.

And I am grateful to family and church, both of whom taught me early to always seek the truth even while practicing a faith far from the conclusions which will be presented here.

1

I Used to Know It All

I was sure I knew it all;
who was bound for heaven and who would be in hell,
how the contradictions in the Bible all fit together when read with guidance from the Spirit and in keeping with our church's exact teaching.
how to fix the US government, end war, and balance capitalism with community,
how to reach every child and teach them anything,
what was true and what was false,
how the world made sense and why it was fair.
Then I heard myself spewing foolishness as wisdom and others doing the same. And, I was repulsed. Such hubris! Each of us know-it-alls living on one small planet on an obscure arm of an unremarkable galaxy but claiming to know all things. Each of multiple branches of my religion claiming to have the correct meaning that everyone else still missed. And, I saw myself in the garden with fruit juice staining my face claiming to know it all, daring to declare myself a god.
Now I know mostly little things;
the love of family,
the importance of children,
the need to live in the circle of a tribe,
the freedom of unknowing,
the joy of being in forest and on rock under birds in flight,

Unified Field Theology

the comfort of not being responsible for all things and all people,
the power each moment to choose behavior that will add to the heaven
or hell experienced in the present by real people,
the beauty of the dance of atoms and stars bracketing the grand
diversity and mysteries of life.
And, I know One Universe which creates, knows, sustains,
and is.
And that is all I need to know.
One is enough.

2

Introduction

Brennan Manning[1] began his wonderful book for those who find faith difficult by clarifying the audience for whom the book was not intended. This work begins much the same. This is not written for the satisfied Christian, content that their faith answers all the questions, or at least all the essential ones. It is not for the person who is comfortable that whatever the Bible says is literally true and all evidence to the contrary is scientific conspiracy or a test of faith placed by God. If your faith is solid, your life is well ordered, and your impact on others is Christ-like, please do not bother with what I intend to share.

This work is for people like me who have found their sure answers replaced by questions and mystery.[2] I do not wish to plant doubts where there are none. The purpose is not to question faith that is healthy for anyone. If you are comfortable in your current theological skin, please do not read this book. I would rather you burn it as heresy, give it to a friend who is struggling, or place it on a back shelf for safe keeping against the day that you find a need for a new perspective on old truths.

Neither is this work for the hardcore atheist. This is not a work of apologetics to overcome the challenges of those offended by faith. I will make no attempt to defend wrongs both past and present done by individuals,

---

1. Manning, *Ragamuffin Gospel*, 11–12.
2. For a parallel account of moving from literal interpretation, through critical questioning, to finding new meaning in the texts based on theology which still maintains belief in a spiritual realm outside of the physical world of science, see Borg, *Convictions*.

groups and governments claiming to do the will of God. I am also offended by any use of faith or claims of holiness to perpetuate suffering in any way. It is part of what drove me to question the sure answers I was taught in my youth.

What will be found here is a collection of contemplations of my own constructions of the universe and our place in it.

- My mind will not be shut off by simplistic arguments that any twentieth-century interpretation of ancient Middle Eastern texts is God's literal record of all that was and is. Science and the remarkable discoveries within my lifetime fascinate and fill me with wonder. I cannot cross them off as lies or tests placed by a loving God.

- My heart rejects the interpretation of the Bible I was raised on which leaves most of humanity in ignorance of the saving knowledge of a loving God. I do not accept arguments which imply or state outright that only those who know and accept a specific list of beliefs and actions are spared from eternal punishment by a God who is also said to be both just and loving.

- My spirit leaps to life when presented with the mysteries of the universe, the evidence of how much remains beyond our current theories, and the way truth dances in the empty space between truths that appear to be opposites.

If you know the life of faith but cannot deny the discoveries of science, this is for you as well. If the fair and loving God of your childhood grew more and more to look like a constantly changing human construction at best and a cosmic sadist at worst, what follows is for you. If you love to contemplate the mysteries, the possibilities, and the contradictions without clear and final answers, this is for you as well. My hope is that it will heal old wounds, affirm present seeking, and empower your own journey of contemplation and a life of freedom. In order to begin, I must do some definition of terms and then address two problems with communication in our time.

Once I gave up the assumptions that I already had all of the answers, I was able to see new possibilities in the discoveries of physics. As the search for a unified theory of everything continues, a pattern has already emerged that reveals many of the characteristics we call God within the nature of what is and can be. I call it *unified field theology*.

3

Terms: How and Why They Will Be Used or Omitted

The following definitions are all from *Merriam-Webster* online. Following is a discussion of how they are used or why they are not used in the essays.

belief

1. a state or habit of mind in which trust or confidence is placed in some person or thing • her *belief* in God • a *belief* in democracy • I bought the table in the *belief* that it was an antique • contrary to popular *belief*

2. something that is accepted, considered to be true, or held as an opinion : something believed • an individual's religious or political *beliefs*; *especially* : a tenet or body of tenets held by a group • the *beliefs* of the Catholic Church

cosmology

1.a. a branch of metaphysics that deals with the nature of the universe

b. a theory or doctrine describing the natural order of the universe

2. a branch of astronomy that deals with the origin, structure, and space-time relationships of the universe; *also* : a theory dealing with these matters

Unified Field Theology

epistemology

1. the study or a theory of the nature and grounds of knowledge especially with reference to its limits and validity

fact

1. a. something that has actual existence • space exploration is now a *fact*

   b. an actual occurrence • prove the *fact* of damage

2. a piece of information presented as having objective reality • These are the hard *facts* of the case.

3. the quality of being actual : actuality • a question of *fact* hinges on evidence

4. a thing done: such as
    a. crime • accessory after the *fact*
    b. *archaic* : action
    c. *obsolete* : feat

5. *archaic* : performance, doing

ontology

1. a branch of metaphysics concerned with the nature and relations of being • *Ontology* deals with abstract entities.

2. a particular theory about the nature of being or the kinds of things that have existence

praxis

1. action, practice: such as
    a. exercise or practice of an art, science, or skill
    b. customary practice or conduct

2. practical application of a theory

theory

1. a plausible or scientifically acceptable general principle or body of principles offered to explain phenomena • the wave *theory* of light

Terms: How and Why They Will Be Used or Omitted

2.a. a belief, policy, or procedure proposed or followed as the basis of action • her method is based on the *theory* that all children want to learn

b. an ideal or hypothetical set of facts, principles, or circumstances—often used in the phrase *in theory* • in *theory*, we have always advocated freedom for all

3.a. a hypothesis assumed for the sake of argument or investigation

b. an unproved assumption : conjecture

c. a body of theorems presenting a concise systematic view of a subject • *theory* of equations[1]

Those trained in philosophy or theology will find each of these areas discussed in the essays that follow. However, a conscious decision has been made to use some and not others. For the most part, I have tried to use terms which are commonly used in general conversation. I have minimized use of terms which might be considered the proprietary vernacular of specific fields of study, such as cosmology, epistemology, ontology, and praxis. Others, such as belief, fact, and theory, are used but deserve some explanation in order to prevent confusion as to their meaning in the essays.

Cosmology deals with the origin, nature, and functioning of the universe. It can be religious or nonreligious. One of my major purposes is to explore the way in which scientific and religious views may be seen as interacting, or at least coexisting, after decades of conflict in conservative Christian thought. This conflict arises from a dualistic approach which has often required acceptance of one and rejection of the other. This either/or thinking has caused discord in US churches and families and great pain for numerous people raised within evangelical organizations. While I will refrain from using this term in order to communicate naturally, many of the essays are deeply concerned with our basic assumptions about cosmology.

Epistemology refers to the way we approach knowledge, or the methods used to obtain knowledge of the world. The methods of the scientist are observation, experimentation, presentation, publication, and replication. The scientific approach depends on the ability to verify evidence through experimentation, either directly or through mathematics, which can be examined and replicated by others in order to eliminate errors and establish the credibility of observations and theories. During my lifetime, this

---

1. See *Merriam-Webster* online, https://www.merriam-webster.com/.

has been viewed as contradictory to the epistemology of religion which claims that knowledge can come directly from divine revelation, the study of divinely inspired texts, or through mystical experience. The gulf between these two views has created rifts between those who believe certain sacred texts interpreted in a specific way to be the only truth and other people, often their own children, trained in scientific methods and unwilling to accept answers which cannot be verified by observation. Many of us have found it impossible to deny evidence that is clearly available when it contradicts interpretations based on revelation.

Ontology refers to what actually is. While epistemology examines how we determine what is, ontology is concerned with the nature of reality. Ontological views have changed dramatically after the rise of science. Earth is found to be far from the center of the universe or even the solar system. Ancient mathematicians were able to deduce that the world was round rather than flat before any known explorers traveled around the globe or out into space to examine and photograph our planet. A religious ontology can contain a spiritual realm separate from the physical based on revealed evidence because it has accepted an epistemology which allows things to be proven by reference to texts believed to have been inspired by God. The scientific community cannot disprove such a realm, but does not confirm its existence because it cannot be studied directly in measurable ways that can be dependably communicated, tested, and observed by others. I will not attempt to disprove faith-based ontologies, but am writing in sympathy with those who cannot accept versions of reality which deny directly observable evidence. Denial of known facts is impossible even as we desire to find greater understanding, or even unity, between the views. I am especially interested in healing relationships between people who see things primarily from different ontological positions.

Praxis is what we do based on what we believe is true. The synonym in common language is practice. My thinking and writing is often focused on praxis, especially in terms of religious beliefs. If we can only verify the veracity of religious claims by referring to texts accepted as revealed truth by people of that faith, then I maintain it is both an allowable and profitable exercise to examine the ways in which those beliefs cause people to behave. Human behavior, both individual and group, can be observed and studied without blind acceptance of external truth. The nonreligious person's observable evidence for the validity of another person's beliefs is often simply how their beliefs cause them to behave in the world including how they respond to others who dare to disagree.

I have chosen not to use these formal terms because of their limited use in conversational English. I find Parker Palmer's book *To Know as We Are Known: Education as Spiritual Journey* to be a brilliant piece of writing with much to say to those in my primary field of education. But, many of my Masters students found it difficult to understand because of its use of formal terms unfamiliar to them. By the time of his book *The Courage to Teach*, Palmer switched to vocabulary more common to teachers and the ideas presented in the text became far more accessible. It is my desire here to examine things carefully and in a respectable way without obscuring the ideas behind vocabulary which would be unfamiliar to many readers. I am not writing for the students of theology and philosophy as much as the people in many other fields who realize there is a problem in the divide between current worldviews. So, I am using language that I believe is most widely accessible. If students of theology or philosophy should also find their way into these ideas, they will know where to apply the labels.

Now to the terms we think we know because we use them, even though we often mean very different things as we speak with each other using the same vocabulary. Even the single-source definitions above include varied and somewhat contradictory meanings based on the context where the word is used and the meaning of the speaker. So, I will try to clarify how these terms are used in my essays.

When I speak about beliefs, I mean those things which people conclude to be true based on the approach they find acceptable. The evangelical Christian believes certain realities about life, meaning, the spiritual realm, and continuation of life after death based on the Bible, specific church doctrines, childhood experience, hope for the future, mystical or emotional personal experiences, and/or other factors peculiar to the individual. As I say elsewhere, it is not my goal to attack the beliefs of those who are comfortable within them and whose life practice is positive. I will, however, distinguish between what we can know by scientific methods that allow others to test our knowledge and theories and beliefs which are particular to individuals and groups and cannot be proven to those who do not accept the primary assumptions of the beliefs. During the various phases of my life, I have often claimed to know things based on what I experienced or believed, but which I could not demonstrate to a nonbeliever unwilling to accept presuppositions of divine revelation or the generalizability of individual experience.

When I speak of facts, I mean statements which can be demonstrated as true regardless of a person's beliefs. That we live on a round planet is now a fact which has been observed and recorded. Common speech, or an actual belief that the sun rises and sets as it revolves around our Earth which appears to be flat observed in the small scale, does not change the fact that we live on a sphere orbiting the sun. I reject some current careless definitions of facts as statements than can be tested for accuracy when those tests have not been done. This leads to the possibility of facts and alternative facts which are equal until testing disproves one and verifies the other. The way I will use the term fact, I mean that which has been demonstrated to be a true statement. For example: under normal conditions if you stand in the middle of your room and release a coin pinched between your fingers without applying any force to it, it will travel to the floor. If we move to explanations of why it does so, our theory of reality will belong to ontology, our methods for studying it will be our epistemology, and our conclusions—if demonstrable and reproducible—will become our theory.

To clarify, I use theory in the scientific sense more than a simple collection of beliefs. If an explanation of some aspect of reality works in different situations under the required conditions, tested by different people, in a way that those in the field can debate and reach agreement, it is a theory. A person hearing strange noises outside their house, observing that their dog seems frightened and forming a mental construction that Bigfoot is visiting their backyard is not the type of conclusion I mean by the word theory. This is significant when we begin any discussion of the relationship between the scientific and religious worldviews. It is very common for people of faith to dismiss the science by pointing out that the idea discussed is *just a theory*. In the scientific sense, this does not equate with saying that an idea is only an assumption or hypothesis. A theory is an explanation that has been tested in multiple ways by different people, many of whom would have been at least as happy to disprove the original idea as to confirm it! Refuting a theory raises the new person to the forefront of discovery of phenomena, confirmation merely confirms the worth of somebody else's work. So, contrary to some common perceptions, ideas in science do not easily rise to the level of theory.

If the religious person asserts at this point that their beliefs have been accepted across centuries and cultures and tested by the perceived

Terms: How and Why They Will Be Used or Omitted

experience of diverse people, I do not object. If they wish to argue that their beliefs rise to the level of ontological theory, I agree. I suspect, however, that the person of faith would be more likely to see description of their beliefs as a theory to be an insult rather than a confirmation since they have already accepted their faith as proven explanation of the nature of the world and its inhabitants.

What I find exciting in all of this—what leads to my conclusion that we can now assert a unified field theology—is that the worldviews of science and faith, which have so often been presented as opposites, have now come together in fascinating ways. I hope that this possibility may reopen dialogue among friends and family members who have found themselves at odds over basic worldviews. I will attempt to be very transparent concerning how I came to see things differently than the beliefs I was raised within in the context of US evangelical fundamentalism. And, except where discussion of ideas requires the vocabulary of a particular field, I will seek to avoid proprietary vernacular.

4

Trouble with Language

As our knowledge of other species has increased, many old perceptions of difference between humans and other animals have been challenged. Other species make and use tools, grieve their dead, arrange their environment in attractive ways, and use language in various forms. Yet, human language remains distinctive in quantity and complexity. Human language, alone in our current knowledge, includes the complexity and nuances required to think and to discuss high-level reasoning and refined theories about the meaning of life and humanity's relationship to the universe. The careful use of a single word or phrase within an assertion of truth, a lyric, or a poem can add layers of significance and connection to other images and writings.

However, we also seem to have reached a dangerous point where words can mean so many things that each person must decide which is intended, or which they choose to apply, as they react to the communication of others. We have reached a point where the inclusion of a single word can cause others to decide if they are for or against an entire argument. Political and religious terms are far from immune to this phenomenon which must be recognized in order to journey into discussions of belief and reality.

If I express support of a safety net for the poor, all that many need to reject my thoughts is to label the idea *leftist*. Then assumptions are made that I support big government, high taxes, regulation of both industry and individual lives, outlawing all personal firearms, and unrestricted abortion on demand. The original meaning of my statement about the advantages of a society which cares for all its members disappears in a rush of other emotionally charged issues.

If I express a view from the right, perhaps the right to own a gun or make one's own decisions about whether to eat snack foods without restrictions from the government, the same thing happens. As soon as a key word allows my thoughts to be labeled *conservative*, assumptions are made that I oppose women's rights, including reproductive decisions, and all regulation of industry whether related to treatment of workers or the environment. It may be further assumed that I support states' rights on issues including those involving basic constitutional issues, and an individual religious right to refuse equal treatment to people outside of my own beliefs.

Religious labels such as Muslim, Jew, or Christian suffer the same fate. If I tell another person that I am a Christian, I cannot assume that they will understand me to mean a person with a lifelong dedication to living according to the sacrificial example of Jesus of Nazareth. I realize full well that they are just as likely to identify me as anti-LGBTQ, intolerant of all other religious beliefs as paths to hell, against all abortion rights, willfully ignorant and intolerant of scientific knowledge and theories about the past and present, and a supporter of any candidate who claims to be pro-life. When a person tries to explain their specific religious stance, the same problem with numerous loaded words appears. As soon as certain markers appear in the conversation, assumptions are made about everything else the person tries to communicate. The responding person needs only to apply a single loaded label to the speaker and everything else they say can be rejected because of convictions and emotions about everything attached to that label.

Communication becomes almost impossible as people hear and assume all the extra meanings they attach to words. Trying to explain each word used to expedite understanding introduces another list of trigger words distracting the other person with reactions to concepts unrelated to the conversation. When all of this is placed within a sociopolitical context which has divided into opposite and antagonistic camps, the problem is multiplied. The size of perceived divisions causes the identification of everyone into categories of friend or foe. It only takes one or two words that serve as markers to block our ability to truly hear the other and have meaningful discussion of views and possible solutions to problems.

I suspect that the shift of numerous individuals in United States society to identifying as spiritual rather than religious is in some ways related to this problem. The very word religious now seems to imply a judgmental attitude to others who do not share the same religious views. Identifying oneself as Baptist, Presbyterian, Catholic, Muslim, or Jewish, attaches the other person's whole list of preconceptions to the speaker. Being *spiritual* can mean anything from actively participating in religion to enjoying time in the woods or appreciating the inner calm of nonreligious meditation. I suspect that some choose this designation to avoid being attached to lists of beliefs they do not hold, or do not want to publicly discuss. I suspect that many are now choosing it because of the same dynamic played out internally. More and more everyday people are weary of the constant public vitriol, of the judgmental aspects of doctrines of churches where they were raised, and of the need to publicly defend views they do not believe but which are attached to their labels.

I know this is true for me. I cannot gather with people in worship of the Jesus I was taught throughout my childhood if I must also endure praise of the military and country which approaches the same level of reverence and worship reserved for God. I cannot sit in the midst of a group claiming to follow the one who taught love of both friend and enemy and listen to justifications of hatred toward other religions, the LGBTQ community, the other political party, the acceptance of scientific facts and theories, or those who have decided that it is easier to draw close to the essence of life by traveling to the woods rather than the cathedral. I have grown weary of the very term Christian due to all the meanings attached to it, many by intentional acts and teachings of the church.

Moving forward will require a strong commitment to converse face to face with others. It will require careful listening to the entirety of what is being said without distraction based on trigger words and phrases. We will need to ask and listen carefully to answers when we do hear words that cause us to suspect other meanings and messages. And maybe it is time to allow the spiritual and mystic to have their place, to acknowledge each other as beings who love life and recognize our smallness in the grandeur of the universe without requiring identification of specific dogmas. Language has begun to fail and divide us. Perhaps it is time to return to being human together in very simple ways—eating together, sitting together in times of happiness and grief, observing the grandeur of the world around us and the beauty of being human—without requiring political and religious language that identifies and divides us.

The ideas contained in these essays are highly susceptible to this problem. It is my hope that they may bring hope to others on similar journeys.

It is also my hope that they may be considered in open discussion which refuses to be derailed by single words or red flag issues. In civil discussion and loving acceptance we can find a way back to greater unity.

5

Paradox: Problem and Promise

Along with the problem of language, we struggle to communicate across differences without an understanding of the power of paradox. Our democratic systems were based on open debate of various views and finding consensus somewhere in the intersection of ideologies, approaches, and goals. The rabbinic tradition contains a wealth of exploring the truth in the interplay of different interpretations of the same sacred texts. However, the twenty-first-century population of the United States seems to have divided into camps unable to entertain the possibility of answers which live only in the space between opposing positions.

Politicians and party true believers tell us that one must believe either in the unrestricted free enterprise of capitalism unencumbered by government or in a nation where every human activity is subject to legislation to protect us from ourselves and the problems of concentrated wealth. When we try to speak across the divide, we are labeled by both sides as soon as we reveal a belief about current issues. Centrists are subject to criticism for disloyalty to both sides, poor understanding of any issue where they reject party lines, and dishonesty for claiming to hold a variety of views. Politicians who decide to run for president abandon any previous statements of agreement or compromise with the other side and speak to the purists at the extremes of each party most likely to work in campaigns and vote on election day.

I have observed the same in the practice and explanation of faith. Fundamentalism requires strict adherence to specific codes of belief which claim to represent the one true interpretation of the Bible, but which may in fact be unique to the individual group and the preferences of a local leader. By contrast, the most liberal expressions of faith demand acceptance of all views including those of other religions. Individual churches exist along the continuum between these positions. But, careful interaction with their beliefs is likely to find the same proclamations of being the proponents of the one true expression of faith. Try to explore the territory where truth is found in the tension between opposites and few evangelical institutions will support the effort. Either there is one expression of truth or all things are true, leaving very little territory for contemplation of paradox.

If we consider the conservative Christianity of my youth and scientific developments since the publications of Charles Darwin, the divide seems complete. Science points to evidence in the geologic record for the age of the planet, the linear progression from simple to complex life-forms, and planetary changes that lasted for enormous periods of time. Conservative faith responds that the book of Genesis, as read and taught by their own favorite authors, is the literal truth of the past given by divine inspiration and revealing that earth has only existed for thousands of years and that each life-form was created independently within the period of one week. Now science points to enormous amounts of data showing the warming of the planet, some as simple to understand as photo evidence of disappearing glaciers, and warns of the predictable results of continued global warming. Conservative Christianity responds that man is not capable of changing the created order outside the will of the Creator and either completely denies the existence of the data or presents the changes of the Anthropocene Era as fitting in God's plan for the planet. Both arguments are used to avoid any restriction of activity which science shows to be contributing to dangerous changes in the climate. Even the term Anthropocene is unacceptable due to its definition based on changes caused by human action. It is easy to reach the conclusion that much of the church, having rejected the theory of evolution, is now likely to reject any evidence or theory that comes from scientific observation and methods. Little room seems left to explore the ways that both traditions can offer meaningful understanding of what it means to be human when their positions seem to be in direct conflict.

As I started my doctoral work at Indiana University, I was fortunate to sit under the teaching of Dr. David Clark. From the first day of class, Dr. Clark encouraged students to be open to new ways of viewing schools as organizations by using aphorisms and counter-aphorisms. We would offer statements about education we believed were accepted by most people without argument. Then, Dr. Clark would invite us into discussions of the truth found in contradictory statements. The claim that schools are for students was countered with the claim that schools are designed for teachers. Suddenly we could see schools as institutions which provide a dedicated space for instruction, colleagues for support, the collection of common resources, personnel to help with troublesome or needy students, and the comfort of a dependable system of teacher income. This also led to consideration of how student learning might be enhanced by escaping the constraints of the classroom for learning in the natural world, museums, libraries, or any number of other settings suggested by the topic under consideration. The truth lies in the paradox. Schools are for children. Woe to any educational professional who would risk proclaiming that the school exists for their own needs rather than those of the students. And yet, much of the design and function of the school is clearly fashioned to benefit and facilitate the work of the adults. One statement is preferred for public consumption. Nevertheless, a sophisticated understanding of the school as an organization is well served by exploring the space between these seemingly opposite statements.

Dr. Ed Buffie invited us into the conflicts between statements concerning leadership and management at the end of the century to explore the way educational leaders could best serve their schools. Dr. Egon Guba took us into the world of constructivism where the only worlds that mattered were the ones in the minds of individuals who sometimes saw things from widely varied perspectives. Dr. Guba taught ways to understand how human beings living and working in the same place experience very different realities. Rather than trying to find the one truth among or between the perspectives, the evaluation model he developed along with his wife, Yvonna Lincoln, provided methods of reflecting these views back to groups in ways that allowed them to interact and create common understandings.[1] These professors, along with authors such as Parker Palmer,[2] have helped me to find great value in paradox.

As I explore the often contradictory statements of truth which often divide us, I constantly look for the way the tension between opposites holds knowledge or wisdom beyond the expressions of either extreme. I grew up loving both faith and science making it highly probable that I would

1. Lincoln and Guba, *Naturalistic Inquiry*.
2. Palmer, *Promise of Paradox*.

have to choose this course or reject one and embrace only the other. I have seen great damage done to individuals and great rifts formed in families as strong adherents of each position try to force others to accept only their view. My essays contain one person's search for the ways truth transcends our theories and dogmas to occupy a space large enough to accommodate apparent opposites. Despite the apparent division of social groups into intolerant camps, I find great promise in the contemplation of the possibilities which abound in paradox.

6

Global Paradigm Shift

One of my prize possessions is a rare copy of *The Emergent Paradigm*, by futurists Peter Schwartz and James Ogilvy. In the 1980s while studying organizational theory and leadership at Indiana University I continually encountered references to this seminal work. Attempting to follow the rules of thorough scholarship, I sought to obtain and read the original. There were few library copies in the North American database and no traveling ones. I was prepared to give up when a classmate suggested calling the publisher directly. That call provided the answer that the publisher was the think-tank SRI and corporations paid fees in the tens of thousands to belong and hundreds more to buy monographs like the one I sought. But, they gave me contact information for one of the authors. He took a very kind interest in my work on new paradigms in education, and a short time later a copy of this amazing work appeared at my home.

In the late seventies awareness grew from work in the physical sciences that personal paradigms control not only how we view the world, but even what we are physically able to see or hear. Schwartz and Ogilvy studied paradigms across a wide variety of disciplines from science to the arts and theology. They found a profound shift in worldviews across the landscape of human thought and research. Their monograph outlined and explained the directions of that change. According to their research, our view of the world was changing away from simple and easy to predict based on previous beliefs that things happened in simple directions of cause and effect. In organizations activity was becoming harder to label as top down, with each person having a distinct place and function in the machine of the organization where they obeyed the directions they were given. The behavior of objects in physics which had been seen as direct with simple forces causing predictable behaviors was entering the current era of events causing each other. During all of this, claims that a human researcher could present an objective description of what was observed were changing to realizations that all human knowledge and research is subjective. Instead of cogs in the great machine, humans were described by Schwartz and Ogilvy as more like portions of a piece of hologram film—not only does the whole contain each piece, but each piece is found to contain the whole![1]

These shifts were happening across the full spectrum of academic disciplines. New knowledge accumulating at rates mankind had never seen before was showing problems and inconsistencies within disciplines and connections across disciplines which required examination and revision. Along with the teachings of Dr. Egon Guba, a pioneer in the transition from traditional research with claims of objectivity and generalizability to situational naturalistic research and evaluation, it all pointed to a world where objective determination of the one truth which superseded all the others was no longer possible or desirable. Common understandings of truth were negotiated realities expressing for a time the conclusions of particular groups of people.

I experienced the liberating realization that many of our observations and conclusions are predetermined by our existing worldviews, and that those beliefs are in flux across disciplines. I had studied worldviews different from my own in the past, but always with an attitude of correctness for my own beliefs wherever conflict appeared. Schwartz and Ogilvy invited me to consider the ways in which other views were equal or superior to my own depending on the variables or theories under consideration.

One of their categories of new thought was that our collective images were becoming more holographic, where each piece contains the entire image. They also showed that old ideas of linear cause and effect where each role can be clearly identified were giving way to complex understandings of the way people and events mutually effect each other.

As the principal of a school for middle school students who had been expelled from public school, I examined the ways that the individual in some way revealed the totality of the organization. My dissertation involved many hours of sitting in interviews with these young people to draw

1. Schwartz and Ogilvy, *Emergent Paradigm*, 13.

out the ways in which their own view of school did and did not reflect the image claimed by those of us in school leadership. One of the key findings was that, while they quite honestly told people that they did not like school, they did possess a strong desire to learn and succeed matching what schools claim as organizational vision and goals. The difference was that the rule-breaking students had reached a point of no longer seeing large public schools as institutions designed in ways that would lead to success for themselves or other students like them. They saw schools' negative actions toward them as a reason to go ahead and act out rather than as a result of their own behavior. Believing that they would be blamed for anything that happened anyway, when they wished to break rules they did so under the assumption that they would be punished for something by the end of the day regardless. The intriguing thing about it all was that their views of school were as true for them as leadership's views of the same institutions were for them. Truth did not lie with one group or the other, but in the lived experiences and resulting views of each group.[2]

During the same period, I was reading widely across varieties of Christian theology. Here were authors who studied the same verses for which I had been taught simple legalistic meanings and they came to widely different conclusions including mystical explanations and universal promises of human acceptance and belonging. In the past, I would have simply categorized new authors and ideas as right or wrong based on my own previous indoctrination. Understanding the existence, variety, and changeability of paradigms made it possible to read each one as an invitation to see life through new lenses without forcing each new idea into an old category.

Schwartz and Ogilvy further state that approaching the world in this way requires:

- An identification of the multiple loci of our perspective, i.e., the psychological locations from which we view and interpret the world.

- An understanding of the process by which we participate in the world—i.e., how we affect others and the world around us—which facilitates the qualities of receptivity and engagement.

- A definition of the boundaries of our partial knowledge, i.e., not overextending the reasonable application of any set of understandings.[3]

---

2. Brown, "We Want to Learn."
3. Schwartz and Ogilvy, *Emergent Paradigm*, 17.

My perspective is heavily influenced by several preferences. First, I was raised to believe that Christianity was the one road to truth, meaningful existence, and eternal bliss. I spent my undergraduate years preparing for a life in evangelical ministry to share that knowledge with others. Second, I grew up in an age of science. I constantly watched on television and read in books and magazines about new discoveries. I watched on television as men landed on the moon and returned safely to earth while others went deeper into the oceans. I always respected this discipline and sought ways to understand areas where science and the specific literal teachings of my faith conflicted. From these two sometimes opposite worldviews, I have both a deep respect for tradition including wisdom literature which has been preserved for millennia and an insatiable desire to know the newest advancements in our scientific knowledge of the world we inhabit. In addition to acquiring a large library, coming to adulthood with growing access to worldwide knowledge through the internet and university access to academic databases resulted in a lifestyle of continuously reading multiple sources across disciplines. *The Emergent Paradigm* gave me confidence that similarities in thought could emerge from careful study in a variety of disciplines. Being fortunate enough to participate in academia through my own degree as well as through teaching and participation in professional organizations has continuously increased my respect for the knowledge and theories expressed by the various disciplines. I can no longer dismiss research or theories which conflict with my prior beliefs. I am drawn to contemplation of the universe which always exceeds our explanations of it, and which I now believe provides a way forward into a unified field theology.

I come to these essays from that platform—as a person who used to believe I knew everything about those parts of the human experience necessary for eternal well-being. I am also fascinated as each new revelation tells us as much about what we do not know as it adds to what we now understand. One of the lenses I now use when examining new material is taken from theoretical physics; does the theory meet the criteria of internal logical consistency.[4] Sometimes new scientific material is openly presented as not yet having met this goal leaving real questions for future research. However, when any system of belief or explanation claims to be complete, I expect the minimum standard of internal consistency to be met.

---

4. I will discuss this concept further in chapter 9, "Twenty-First-Century Worldviews."

7

My Own Path

I was born in Evansville, Indiana, in 1956. While we lived in the city, the area remained largely agricultural. Factories in town provided dependable jobs for men like my father who worked to provide comfortable lives for their families in the rising middle class. Races were mostly segregated in daily life, in school, and in church. Television was new and programming reflected the values and beliefs of my conservative world. When it did not, we were not allowed to watch.

I grew up in a fundamentalist evangelical Presbyterian church. Looking back now, that combination alone should have been warning of conflicts to come. However, I knew nothing about other worldviews, the larger world of theology, or the diversity over time in church history. My mother taught Sunday School for adults and would spend hours with stacks of Bible translations and commentaries to make sure that what she presented to her class on Sunday was the right explanation, the only right explanation. We prepared the bread and grape juice for communion Sundays in our kitchen at home. My father, who was a printer by trade, ran the church's old press and prepared the weekly bulletins for service. I spent many hours reading or napping on a small church pew that now resides in my home. We knew the truth about God, creation, history, salvation and the future and we supported missionaries to share that truth in other countries.

I first went to the front of the church to accept personal salvation at age six after experiencing a strong positive emotional reaction to a Sunday sermon. Later when I was twelve, a missionary couple came to share stories about their work. I wanted what they had and was excited about the life they described. I again accepted the invitation to become a Christian with family and church agreeing that I now had sufficient adult understanding to make the decision. From that day through much of my adult life I intended to become a Christian missionary, either at home or abroad.

By high school I understood enough to know that there were many other worldviews. I devoured each book produced by Francis Schaeffer or his wife, Edith. I appreciated his discussion of views other than my own within a framework which also reassured me that my own views were still the truth.[1] I attended national tours they held twice, including one with coauthor C. Everett Koop which helped to launch the pro-life movement.[2] For a time, the work of Francis Schaeffer assured me that the challenges to my childhood worldview had been considered and answered.

I attended then Indiana State University at Evansville, a state school cheap enough for my scholarships to more than cover my expenses with no student loans. After college, I planned to work for the evangelical organization Young Life and attend their Bible college. I finished college with that plan still intact, but also having encountered new ways of looking at the world. Professor Donald E. Pitzer became a lifelong mentor as well as my instructor in US history. Driving across country to attend conferences on the history of US communal societies, and later in senior coursework in US intellectual history, we would spend hours discussing newly discovered knowledge and its implications for reexamining worldviews. My beliefs and plans held, but a window had been opened for a lifetime of considering new possibilities and reflecting on constructions carried forward from childhood.

During doctoral studies at Indiana University, I sat under the instruction of Egon Guba. Egon and his wife, Yvonna Lincoln, were pioneers in the field of naturalistic inquiry. He taught me methods for evaluating organizations and conducting other research by exploring other constructions of reality. Sociology and anthropology have long understood this as the difference between emic and etic views. Dr. Guba pushed things further and eliminated all claims of unbiased objective determination of truth. In the worldview he taught, there are only constructions, no possibility of eliminating the influence of one's own constructions, and no single truth to be found outside of human constructions. By that time, I was running

---

1. Schaeffer, *How Should We Then Live*.
2. Schaeffer and Koop, *Whatever Happened*.

a school for expelled middle school students and obtaining methods for seeing the world through their eyes as clearly as possible was invaluable. Their hope for finding a path toward success in society depended entirely on what made sense in their view, not mine. It worked. It also took me further along the path of realizing that I was not the holder and disseminator of one truth for all people.

Since then I have continued the studies, reflections and contemplations discussed in these essays. It has often been painful, as any departure from acceptance of one narrow view of the truth brings the possibility of rejection from my faith community. The area where I live remains very conservative in politics, social policy, and religion. Isolating oneself from evangelical Christianity as the one and only truth, can easily mean isolating oneself from the larger community. One of my desires to share the following reflections is the possibility of finding a new community of people who find themselves on similar journeys.

8

Know

I used to know so much. At least I thought I did. I knew how the world started and how it would end. I knew the meaning of all of history and how it related to me. I knew which countries were good and who the bad guys were. I knew exactly what *being good* and *being bad* meant.

I no longer claim to possess such universal certainty. And it isn't just the diminishing capacity of my mind to remember that is at work. It is the diminishing ability to rule out all other possibilities.

For all our posturing, neither faith nor science truly allows us to peel back the veil and know with no possibility of error everything about the time before human comprehension or to predict the end of all things. Some of my Christian friends will already be offended. They will respond that we know because the Bible tells us. But, that is a choice to believe. We cannot verify it. We cannot convince others of our views using testable facts and evidence. And it is views, not view, because there is great diversity of interpretation even among those who claim to believe the same book. Belief in writings handed down from antiquity is an act of faith, not an act of knowing. Belief that current events in some way match portions of those writings interpreted as predicting the end is a matter of matching observations to faith. Previous generations were just as sure when they matched those same writings to events in their own times. Those who reject the Bible as the exclusive source for information, also reject the conclusions because there is no way to produce acceptable evidence outside of belief in the beliefs.

We do not know. We choose to believe. We choose to act as though we believe. Too often we choose to behave in ways that contradict what we claim to believe. Then our behavior becomes the observable evidence available to others. The disconnect between proclaimed doctrine and behavior is one of the issues that gives me pause about many of my experiences in the Midwestern US church. If we knew final truth, with no doubt and with full evidence of fact and consequence, would we choose to twist those beliefs to match what is convenient or attractive? And yet, I often watched doctrine taught as eternal truth change when it became personally inconvenient.

We do not know. Faith is not required to believe something that can be fully verified and known.

We do not know. We choose.

We weigh the evidence available to us. We weigh the apparent worth of human explanations of meaning in the universe. We weigh the evidence of the fruit of living out various beliefs. And we choose.

We know our own experience and we place meanings upon that experience. But, we do not possess the experience or share the exact same constructions as others. When they choose to share, we try to understand. We approximate the feelings and understandings of their experience, but it is not our own and we do not fully know it. And, our experiences are not proof of anything to others. They know their own paths and their own interpretations of what they have seen and felt. We share with each other in order to enrich each other, but we do not truly know.

Many of us can no longer maintain the unshakable position that we know one set of truths that fit all people in all times. We choose to believe; we construct meaning out of the evidence we understand and out of experiences often beyond our comprehension. Hopefully, we live in ways that are empowered by the beliefs we choose and examine both our behavior and our beliefs as life adds wisdom to our journey.

If a person has faith that their beliefs are absolute and final truth, I hope those beliefs serve them well and enrich their lives. The rest of us watch to see if the effects are evidence for or against their claims. Yet, faith is precious and I do not seek to harm it.

But it *is* faith, precisely because we do not know. Only with acceptance of our diversity can we hope to meet in a unified field of common humanity.

9

Twenty-First-Century Worldviews

> People say that what we're all seeking is a meaning for life. I don't think that's what we're really seeking. I think that what we're seeking is an experience of being alive, so that our life experiences on the purely physical plane will have resonances with our own innermost being and reality, so that we actually feel the rapture of being alive.[1]

Two worldviews dominated the world I was taught and taught to others. The scientific view was based on that which is observable and replicable as fact. The religious view was based on what was revealed and believed by faith to be fact. When the observed conflicted with what was taught as revealed truth, choices had to be made. The most conservative of US Christians, the group I know best by experience, clung to the teachings of revelation in the face of ever-increasing observable evidence. Other religious people found ways to adjust their worldviews, approach their ancient texts in new ways, and incorporate what science revealed through observation. Many people chose to completely reject any world of faith contrary to demonstrated fact.

When science explored the meaning of the fossil record and developed new theories on the development of biological diversity, the contrast to belief based on literal interpretation of ancient text and choices of faith

---

1. Campbell, *Power of Myth*, 12.

appeared to be a clear line of difference. Religions chose to progress or stand still, even to retreat into imagined ages of surety from the past. Science marched forward and conflict appeared in many ways unavoidable. Still, for a time science dealt with replicable observations of fact while religion depended on loyalty to doctrines of revealed truth.

Then science reached new frontiers. Study of the universe reached levels where theory became impossible to test in the lab. We cannot look through the wormhole to see what is on the other side. We cannot observe any universe other than our own when multi-universe theory seems a logical explanation for the edges of our knowledge. Science reached a point where confirmation by replicated experimentation can no longer be used as the criteria for acceptance or rejection of new hypotheses. And a new form of examination and language emerged. Scientific inquiry at the edges of human knowledge is now examined for "internal logical consistency."[2]

If a theory works across all parameters by the same rules, it is plausible. If a theory reaches points where the math or explanations of its physics contradict other aspects an internal inconsistency has been found. The theory is then deemed to be in error. Proponents of the theory may find ways to resolve the inconsistency rather than reject their view of the universe. When the inconsistency cannot be resolved, other theories to explain the universe are considered superior.

As I begin to write about how I view the universe, truth, and man's place in space and time, I will need to explain why my views have moved away from the ones I grew up believing were divine revelation. This may offend some who hold those views while providing mental and spiritual oxygen to others who know something is wrong but do not know where we turn for new and viable worldviews. Our humanity and the same needs that drove us to accept old beliefs will continue to cause us to desire affirmation of what we have known as *good* and rejection of things considered *evil*. We will see where the journey takes us, but the measure I will use rather than desire for certain types of explanations is whether a view of the universe has *internal logical consistency*.

If a worldview contradicts its own definitions and explanations it fails this test. To be feasible within the thought systems of the twenty-first century, a worldview will need to remain consistent with its own claims. This is the test that I will use as I explore the way my own beliefs in the US fundamentalist evangelical paradigm imploded. The same measure will

2. Popper, *Logic*, 72.

apply to alternative ways of seeing life, the wisdom and teachings of ancient texts, and the place of humanity in the universe which I call unified field theology.

10

The Narrative Implodes

My relationship with the American evangelical narrative began very early as my parents were highly active in church and youth evangelism. What caused me to make a personal commitment to beliefs was the testimony of visiting missionaries. Tales of Africa, danger, and people in need convinced me at a young age that I would devote my life to similar pursuits. I chose elementary education as my college major because it seemed the closest to the local public university's choice for a general liberal arts degree. The plan was to work for Young Life and do graduate work in their Bible institute. I saw it as a life career choice. As recently as ten years ago my retirement plan was still to move into mission service on a foreign field.

Still looking backward, the seeds of change were planted very early. Part of the urgency in the evangelical narrative was that this God who exemplified love to those who knew him and justice for the whole of creation, could tolerate no sin. This left all those who were not Christians in peril of eternal damnation because they would die in their sins never having known there was a choice.

I remember one local evangelist, a dear man who sincerely believed every word he uttered, preaching about the pain he felt watching cars go down the highway realizing how many contained people who did not know the truth and whom he would never meet in order to help them be saved. I remember feeling a pang of discord having been taught that the all-present God also saw and loved those same people. As a child, I could accept explanations that God's ways are not our ways,[1] or that all deserve to die and be punished; the miracle is that some are saved.[2] Adult understandings of words like love and justice do not easily endorse these types of caveats for anything so serious as the eternal destiny of most of mankind.

THE NARRATIVE I WAS TAUGHT

As I grew, the narrative gained complexity as the whole of the Protestant Bible was woven into a continuous history of God's interactions with man from a literal six-day creation through the cross and resurrection of Jesus Christ onward into a day of future judgment and finally to Christ's earthly rule and perfection. The very first people were taught directly by God until they rebelled in sin and became separated. Mankind grew and expanded in both population and depravity until God once again reduced the population to a single faithful family through a global flood. Scientific evidence for landmasses having previously been under water and theories for how a rain and flood of such magnitude could occur were proudly shared along with the confirmation that cultures with no knowledge of the saving Jesus still remembered the flood.

Humankind again multiplied and grew in hubris until men literally (everything was literal) tried to reach heaven through construction of a physical tower. God dispersed them by creating the variety of human languages. Eventually God choose a man to be the father of those who would receive special revelation of truth and be enabled to have relationship again with the divine. This man did not act like the rest of the narrative says we are to act, but all that is explained away as evidence of how wonderfully God uses us despite our flaws. From him and his descendants the tribes of Israel emerged. Somehow, they knew enough to obey this God of justice at least part of the time. Then famine struck and they moved to Egypt where they eventually became slaves. After hundreds of years their cries of pain caused God to raise up the hero Moses and finally the narrative includes God giving the people written rules for life and worship.

Somehow as a child, I could accept it as logical that these instructions were given at the time when God established a new nation devoted to him and designed to be a beacon for the world. A large part of this acceptance came from the teaching that "God said it. I believe it. That settles

1. Isaiah 55:8–9.
2. Romans 3:23–24.

it."[3] Questions of how a just God could allow all those generations to live and die facing judgment without clear knowledge of the holy requirements were simply dismissed.

After long centuries of faithful and unfaithful leaders, victory and exile, the narrative reached the events recorded in what Christians call the New Testament and Jesus arrived proclaiming that while all the law stands for all time, it is love which saves. He lived and died as the perfect sacrifice for all man's wrongs so that all the world could be saved. He then returned to heaven where he is one and the same with the God of the Old Testament. The church grew and spread, becoming more and more anti-Jewish (for some reason one of the only parts I never accepted) and proclaimed that it is belief in this Jesus, repentance from sin, and baptism that adopts one into the family of God. And for evangelicals, it is only through this method that man can be right with God and not suffer eternal punishment. The older established Catholic Church was ridiculed for placing priests, church teachings, and even the buying of indulgences into this process that was meant to be freely given to all.

This would be my life's work. To reach as many as possible with news that there is more to life than is apparent, that there is a God who loves and wants relationship with them, and that the stakes of refusal are incredibly high. I believed it. I taught it. I trained others to teach it. I am ordained in an evangelical denomination. But I now find that it has all fallen into a heap of misinterpretation, misrepresentation, and exploitation.

PERSONAL CRISIS AND REAFFIRMATION

There was a moment of existential crises in my early adulthood when faith and hope collapsed and then were somehow affirmed.

My wife and I had three beautiful girls and then lost three in a row during pregnancy. The third, Lindsey, was past the normal danger points. We were assured everything was going to be fine this time. Then her heart simply stopped. We had to wait for her to be still born. It did not happen. My wife had to go in the hospital for them to force her delivery. Since it was a Catholic hospital, and thus pro-life, my grieving, suffering wife was forced to sign papers guaranteeing that this was not an elective abortion. The hospital gave me supplies to baptize my stillborn daughter, which I did. We had a funeral and buried her. But, my wife was destroyed. None of those

3 Stewart, "God Said It."

Bible verses of promise came true. Her prayers were not answered. It didn't work. A pastor came to our home to help us deal with it all. He listened briefly and told my dear heartbroken wife the answer was for her "to get off the pity potty," accept it, and move on. I threw him out of our house. Other more caring friends from church gave us a famous book by a Jewish author explaining that there are things God just cannot change.[4] We were given no evangelical Christian answers unless it was the heartless statement that our faith was not strong enough to move this mountain. It did not work.

I sat downstairs in my office journaling. I decided I had been raised on lies and old superstitions. My secular professors had been correct. The universe occurred by chance, and while certain properties of movement and interactions could be explained, the bottom line was that it was all meaningless. You are born. You experience enough joy to expect good things. And, the reality of life's pain crushes you. You die. Then I experienced what seemed to be an audible voice that challenged me. "So, what will you do?" My deep heart response was, "I will take care of anybody who is close to me in this pain and darkness. I will do everything I can to make things better for anyone chance brings close to me." Then the reply, "Isn't that what I taught you all along? If you can believe that, you can believe."

It became my life's call. I would take care of anybody I could. It became my professional life as I ran a school for children the other schools refused to serve. And somehow for a long season, I allowed it to answer all of the problems with the version of truth I had taught and would continue to teach. In the course of time I was lucky enough to travel to Africa and to China as part of Christian mission teams. I visited the Lakota Reservation at Pine Ridge and the landfill slums of Mexico. And my largest objection to the traditional narrative grew as I was exposed to the number of people who live and die outside the reach of these teachings.

INTERACTING WITH SCIENCE

Science also gradually became more and more problematic for me after my undergraduate years. Originally, I had materials from evangelical circles showing how science that contradicted our version of life including the six-day creation was simply wrong. The steady state universe I had been taught as a child was suddenly replaced by the big bang theory which surprisingly confirmed that there had been a moment when nonexistence changed to

---

4. Kushner, *When Bad Things Happen*.

existence—for me that seemed to affirm creation. I remember the moment when an undergraduate professor who became my lifelong mentor said that the universe now appeared more like a giant thought than a machine! We were right! The explanation of the universe which I had been taught said that God thought it, spoke it, and it was. Never mind that evangelicals were claiming a five thousand year-old universe while science produced evidence of numbers too large to imagine. They were just wrong on the methods that were giving the numbers. But, knowledge does not stay static and new knowledge requires reexamination of many things we are sure of before the encounter.

As I dared to learn more of the evidence of the physical world, the evangelical explanations required rejecting the clear evidence of science. Intelligent observation of the planet required either rejecting the literal creation story, turning biblical days into entire geological epochs, or recognizing that the conflicting accounts of creation in Genesis are ancient myths on the origin of life. Mainstream denominations, which I had been raised to see as liberal or even heretic, accepted the science and looked to the ancient text as myth or prescientific understanding of the world. But the evangelicals that I continued to worship with, insisted that faith required accepting what was written as literal truth no matter what science said. This became an issue almost too large to ignore. I love the life of the mind, the exploration of the world, the pursuit of evidence wherever it leads and the sheer joy of sudden understanding of things one never knew. Asking me to turn off my brain in order to accept faith, made it more and more difficult for me to sit in their churches and listen to their sermons. Deliberate ignorance is hard for me to tolerate.

COLLAPSE OF THE NARRATIVE

But, the camel's straw for me lies within the teaching of US evangelicals far more than in external challenges. Granted that continued education and the development of more informed lenses made it harder and harder to accept naive readings of ancient texts, it is the internal inconsistency of the literal narrative that I can no longer accept.

1. The original sin was committed by a man and woman who had no knowledge of the difference between good and evil until *after* the act occurred.

2. There is no account of what God required of humans or how they were supposed to know it as generations multiplied until the God of love and justice decided to kill them all in the great flood.

3. After choosing a faithful family, the world was again allowed to populate with no recorded instructions of how humans could find connection with this Creator.

4. God punished and dispersed mankind again at the tower of Babel. While evangelicals may claim that this is so the earth will be filled with the worship of the Creator, there is no explanation of how the people spread around the planet were supposed to know what that meant.

5. God again selected an individual, commanded him to leave the land of his birth without teaching anyone there the ways of this God, punished people with no knowledge of divine law when this man tricked them due to his own fears, and established him as the head of God's family on earth.

6. People continued to function on what can only be assumed was oral tradition containing stories of divine dreams until they found themselves in bondage to another kingdom.

7. When they were freed, they were told that what God gives to man is law for proper behavior and were left to practice that for centuries.

8. As their nation was established, God's way included complete massacre of men, women, children, and even animals that happened to already live on the land they were to claim.

9. Then they were told to be a beacon in the world and to share blessings including the knowledge of their God with all. But, they failed to remain true to these teachings within their own culture or to share them with others.

10. Suddenly with the arrival of Jesus of Nazareth we are told that the real measure has been the heart and not behavior all along.

11. His followers were told again that God loved the whole world and they were to go and make disciples among all people.

12. So this loving and just God punishes people for what they have never been taught, sets up his own country while again teaching them something other than the true path to life, appears in person to only that

people group and those who happen to be in their area, and leaves the work of spreading this teaching of the truth to human beings who assume the people in contact with Mediterranean trade and culture represent the entire world.

13. The people of the far East, sub-Saharan Africa, and the American continents are completely missing from access to the revelations of God until the era of empire and conquest when the gospel was accompanied by genocide and land theft.

14. Those who do not somehow find God and worship him properly in the midst of all of this ignorance and outright misdirection are condemned to eternal suffering.

There is no internal consistency for this worldview. This warlike, favorite choosing God, willing to ignore most of humanity while misleading those who are called by his name and then send the vast majority of creation into punishment, cannot be the ultimate expression of either love or justice. The central figure in this American evangelical narrative fails to meet the standards of basic human dignity. The entire thing caves in upon itself leaving nothing beyond man worthy of worship.

11

The Dark Side of a Shepherd God

One of the flaws in US evangelical theology which continues to concern me is this idea that a just and loving God would interact and reveal the path to salvation to only people living near the Mediterranean Sea. I will return to this later as the same writings appear very differently when allowed to be the oral histories, myths, and traditions of a particular group of people describing their interactions with the universe and the unknown. However, it seems like an obvious flaw in the interpretation I followed for most of my life that the whole populations of North and South America, sub-Saharan Africa, Australia, and the Far East would be allowed to live and die with no knowledge of the revelations to Israel or the emerging Christian church. It is not logical that a just or loving God would allow these people to live and die in ignorance, and even worse condemn them to the eternally consuming fire of hell, for not living by beliefs they never knew.

As I was contemplating this, I began to wonder what kind of person would compare to such a God. How would society respond to a person who would intentionally bring forth life intended only for death. My mind goes to evangelical furor over those who would start the development of a fetus and then abort it. I think also of the apprehension toward any science that might lead to producing human duplicates as a source of donor organs and longevity. Surely, people who hold these views would not also love a God that begins life only to destroy it.

Then it came to me. There are people we honor for continuously managing the increase and growth of new lives for the sole purpose of death and consumption. They are called farmers and ranchers. Living as omnivores, we have no problem with those who breed life to be used for our pleasure and consumption. Could that reality affect our willingness to accept a God who does the same? Could it have been a psychological factor at the time the writings we call the Bible were produced?

And there it is. The Bible continuously refers to God as a shepherd in the books of both the Christian Old and New Testaments—and the Jewish Torah and Talmud. The original preference between people attributed by God is for the son of Adam who kills and sacrifices animal life over the son who brings only plants cultivated for food. The original covering of man's nakedness is done by God through the killing of animals. As the patriarchs arrived and grew in understanding of this God, animal sacrifice became a normal and regular practice lasting until the destruction of the Jerusalem temple in AD 70.

The faith of my youth emphasized the loving care and constant protection of the shepherd. Churches displayed images of Jesus carrying a lamb on his shoulders and surrounded by sheep. We were taught how the shepherd slept in the opening of the sheep enclosure and was the protector of the flock from any danger. We were taught how the shepherd will go in search of a single lost sheep as an example of deep love for each and every member of the flock. We never dwelt on the idea that those sheep were produced and protected not only for sheering, but also for consumption in the home and for casting on the sacrificial fires.

And, it occurs to me that a people comfortable with a God who sought the burning of valued livestock upon the alter, would not be deeply troubled by a God who produced some life for fellowship and special status and others for destruction. Total annihilation of people living in areas God wishes to give to his favorites is recorded, read, and taught with little evidence of concern for the lack of love or justice in such actions. I know the Christian theological discussions claiming that the people destroyed had become completely wicked, and had been given time to follow the correct path although there is no clear teaching on how they would have known what that path was, before a just God ordered their destruction. Then, the part of the narrative which says to destroy even the youngest children and the animals is brushed aside before it can cause any great consternation with how the infant or the farm animal could have any real guilt deserving of destruction.

A shepherding people would understand a worldview in which some life exists to live in blessing and careful attention while other life is seen as threatening or is set aside for consumption and therefore to be destroyed. Even the favored best of the flock belonged to God when the time for sacrifice arrived. The texts also tell us the ancients went as far as participating in rituals sacrificing their own children to please other gods. Such a culture could logically accept a God who behaved as they behaved and see that God as just and loving. It is normal human psychology to see our own behaviors, and those of others who are like us, as correct and acceptable.

The God of these people is no vegetarian. From the very first generation described in Genesis, some life comes into being to be valued and others for destruction on our behalf. The people understand that they breed some animals to live a full life and others to be consumed in the home or upon the altar. Why would they waiver when presented with teachings of a God who does the same? Some people come into being for God's fellowship, pleasure, and service while others are born destined to destruction.

Before I leave this metaphor of a shepherd God who produces some for companionship and some for destruction, an even more irreverent thought arises. If this is an accurate view of the Divine, then what is salvation? Is it not the process and behaviors required to become a valued and cherished pet rather than wait for the day when one becomes the entrée?

Of course, the people at the time of the writings had no knowledge of the other continents or their occupants. However, as I sit here in the twenty-first century, I have been privileged to travel to China and Africa. I was born and live in North America and have met and been taught by descendants of the empires of Turtle Island. I remain an omnivore, so I have not totally rejected the practice of raising animals to be consumed by humans. But, it makes no sense to me to revere an image of God that presents the divine source and destination of all things in the same way.

The image of Jesus with a lamb on his shoulders is no longer comforting when that lamb may be on its way to be burned on the alter or stewed in the family kitchen. All metaphors can be stretched too far. Perhaps I play too loosely with this one. I doubt that any author of the texts we call the Bible or the Torah contemplated things directly in this way. But, it makes sense to me that the practices of their daily lives and the stories they held as holy would make it possible to revere a God who saved some and ignored total populations of others.

I do not believe the power of the universe plays favorites with people, galaxies, or sheep. Life is. We know life as it exists where we are. We have no idea how many other life-forms may exist in the universe. Everything comes from and returns to the same universal background field. I do not believe it has a chosen flock favored above all others. It is up to us to decide if we look into the vastness of the cosmos in wonder. It is up to us whether we treat other life, at the bare minimum other human beings, as our equals in existence or inferiors subject to our decisions to wage war or deny basic resources. If there are any shepherds, they are us—not some external God.

12

Gossamer Chains

> O Sinner! Consider the fearful Danger you are in:
> 'Tis a great Furnace of Wrath, a wide and bottomless
> Pit, full of the Fire of Wrath, that you are held over
> in the Hand of that God, whose Wrath is provoked
> and incensed as much against you as against many of
> the Damned in Hell: You hang by a slender Thread,
> with the Flames of divine Wrath flashing about it, and
> ready every Moment to singe it, and burn it asunder;
>
> and you have no Interest in any Mediator, and nothing to lay hold of to save yourself, nothing to keep off the Flames of Wrath, nothing of your own, nothing that you ever have done, nothing that you can do,
>
> to induce God to spare you one Moment.[1]

I'm not sure I need to say any more about this topic. And yet, it remains strong in my contemplations. This may be because I suspect reading some of my recent thoughts will cause friends and relatives still holding to this type of theology to fear for me. I would spare them that pain if I could.

What kind of God is this who holds those created in his own image by threads while flames reach up and about them? What kind of preacher

---

1. Edwards, "Sinners in the Hands of an Angry God," 16.

Unified Field Theology

is this who sees himself outside of the picture, as if he has some special vantage point for viewing both this God and these poor souls? How is this gospel good news of a loving God? How does this image match the beautiful imagery of a God willing to become flesh, dwell among men, suffer all they suffer, and take their suffering fully upon himself? To be brief, I reject it.

When I first learned of the sermon many years ago, I found it quaint and old fashioned—the kind of sermon few would preach in more recent times. But, I did not disagree with it. I was raised fully within a tradition that said those outside of Christianity were doomed to eternal suffering in the flames and remained alive moment by moment only by the grace of God that they might have time to repent and be saved. While those within my tradition believed our own security to be eternal, we truly believed that the fate of all others was as fragile as the cord of life itself. At any second, they might face the moment of the cord's breaking and their eternal condemnation to suffering. Until finally, the horror of such a world made it unbelievable to me.

After years of practicing what evangelicals call a personal relationship with God, I do not know this God who would create most of mankind to live and die hanging on this precarious thread. I do not know this God who would allow them to come into existence in places with no knowledge of his narrow path to salvation and pass into eternal separation because they were born in the wrong years and the wrong places. I do not know these people who, while living life by better creeds of hospitality than practiced in my own culture—kind and gentle and willing to teach me their ways when we meet—remain so evil that a just God would hold them by a thread he will eventually cut and drop them into the fire.

Something happened. I stepped outside the picture and over to Edwards's magic viewing station and found the picture absurd and abhorrent. Having stepped outside the circle to view the image, I did not wish to be bound to the kind of God in this sermon by any thread be it gossamer or golden. I have no common ground with this God who plays with life and eternity. I love the people I have met from other cultures and beliefs. Our common humanity binds us as brothers in a universe beyond imagination filled with apparent chaos which indeed makes life fragile and temporary. I would never hold them in harm's way. I have a lifelong aversion to those who justify war and killing based on our religious and cultural differences. How can I accept a God who would play with them on the end of a string?

A spider's thread may be woven into amazing designs and be beautiful to behold. Yet it remains a device to capture and devour. I look back now at the remains of my own thread and it is revealed as a heavy chain. It bound me to a negative view of the world and of God. I learned too much about how it has been used to justify man's inhumanity to man. I learned too much of the beauty found outside this theater of pain. And now, I leave this magic thread behind as a slave leaves the shackles. I will live in the grandeur and wonder of the universe that is and take my chances here in the field of unity with my brothers and sisters.

13

Good and Evil

In most theology, both conservative and liberal, good is expressed in thoughts and behaviors consistent with the rules given by God. Evil is anything contrary to, or outside of, the intentions of God for humans. Legalistic doctrine places greater emphasis on statements of God's will for behavior expressed as law and on punishment for those who behave differently. More liberal approaches emphasize love of God and neighbor and see the biblical behavioral mandates as guidance for harmonious human behavior. But religious definitions of good and evil are all based on information from beyond the natural world.

One of the major problems is a lack of internal logical consistency in either belief or practice. Rules from thousands of years ago that match our desired lifestyles are emphasized and people claim that they live by them, or that they at least do their best to obey within individual and group circumstances. Rules, such as not eating certain foods, that appear silly to us are simply ignored. Ancient pronouncements forbidding behaviors outside of our own personal or cultural desires are used to label other people and their behaviors as evil. And yet, these are all from the same ancient texts with no caveat provided in the source for choosing which rules apply across time. My current study of Jewish tradition includes an openness to change over time, but the tradition I was raised in did not.

In my own religious life, I have watched the rules change. When I was a child, our conservative church taught that all sex before marriage was sin; marriage was holy and permanent rendering all divorce as sin; alcohol was not to be consumed even when we celebrated the wine of Jesus' blood in communion; and the Bible was to be taken literally in everything that it affirmed. Yet, my parent's generation, who came to maturity before effective birth control, often had children born well within the first ten months of marriage. The sin was no longer a sin if the couple got married before their families felt shame. When a much loved daughter of the church was being beaten by her husband, divorce became acceptable. When a well-liked man of the church abused his family, everyone continued to pretend they did not know and the wife was supposed to remain faithful. Alcohol turned out to be OK to drink at a social event where it would be rude to refuse the host or if nobody admitted drinking in conversations at church. To include one of today's most divisive issues, gay church members were also accepted and loved as long as everyone pretended not to know they were gay. While we clung to literal reading of texts like Genesis in spite of all scientific evidence, it turned out that what was good and evil in practice was determined by what we found possible or attractive.

Beyond inconsistency in our use of the texts for our own lives, we apply them differently according to who is acting. In the United States, we pay constant homage to all who serve in the military. They are honored not only at political events and national holidays of remembrance, but at every sporting event and in many worship services. Current expression tends to indicate that a person is heroic and worthy of praise simply by taking the oath and donning the uniform of US military service. However, one who is born in a different country, loyal to their homeland, and willing to serve militarily is evil if our two nations are in conflict. Good and evil are reduced to whether a person is defined as us or them—protector or threat to us. Some construct complicated interpretations of Bible passages to say that the United States is now the nation expressing God on earth. Our country is presented as God's agent, because we are the friend and protector of the post-World War II nation of Israel making our own violent presence in the world acceptable.

To push the idea further, killing another human is wrong. However, it is OK for the military to kill to protect the interests of our nation as discussed above. And it continues. A person who takes the life of another citizen is a murderer. And, we use the Bible to say the penalty for murder is death. However, the agent of the state can kill another person who has been rendered helpless because we have labeled the servant of the state as good, and the person convicted of murder as evil. Then we extend it further and give both officers of the state and individual citizens the right to strike first. In the recent past the standard for this was clear evidence that the other person was a threat to our lives. In many states the standard has now become internal, giving us the right to kill another person if we *fear* that they are a danger to us or to others. Even the retaliatory justice of ancient law had no such extension. One can also find no cities of refuge in modern practice where the person guilty of manslaughter can escape judgment by clinging to the mercy of God. That idea is foreign to even those who claim our acts are based upon the texts that require both to exist. The teachings of Jesus take us all the way to the opposite. Jesus taught his followers to love enemies, turn the other cheek, pray for those who persecute them, and even to die without resorting to violent response.

Yet, the loudest defenders of the right to carry deadly weapons and use them against any perceived threat are most often found among those who claim to be defenders of biblical faith as followers of Jesus. We ignore the evidence of how the law is more likely to find minorities guilty of murder and sentence them to death and more likely to find that white males acted according to these vague definitions of self-defense. We brush aside evidence that the government often lies and distorts evidence in order to gain convictions of those accused—in spite of the fact that many people have been found innocent of the crime even *after* being executed by the state. And we demand our rights to kill whenever we consider killing necessary in order to feel safe. It is not consistent with the religious texts, or in application across social groups. Evangelical Christianity in the United States continues to assert that its beliefs and teachings are directly from God. Nonetheless, my own experiences with faith in practice lead me to conclude that good and evil are often reduced to our desires and who we identify as part of *us* or one of *them*. I see no consistent logical system capable of proving our practiced definitions to exist outside of our own constructs.

14

Blaming Those Hurt by the Church

I have often seen this same sort of thinking result in callous statements and behaviors toward those who are hurt by actions of the church or faith-based organizations. There is a tendency among Christians to proclaim that people who reject God based upon the behavior of people, were never trusting God in the first place. It is the kind of apparent logic that seems to elegantly identify the nature of a problem but actually discounts both the viewpoint and value of the offended person.

Frankly and bluntly, I call foul. I want to call it something earthier and easily found on Midwestern farms, but I'll stick with foul.

My problem is that faith organizations I know want it both ways. They freely claim to speak for God, to provide the true interpretation of divine texts, and to be the hands and feet of God in the present age. When things go smoothly, they are more than happy to tell you that they represent God as his physical visible presence through the indwelling of the Holy Spirit. Try to say that you are fine with God without attending their ceremonies and contributing to their budget and they will tell you it is not an option. You must participate in the collective and each organization will claim they are the correct place to attend because they most accurately represent God. But, let something go wrong—let people be hurt both emotionally and spiritually—and new verbiage emerges.

Suddenly the person who has been harmed is the problem. The upset people are focusing too much on humans who never claimed to be perfect, instead of leaning into the perfection and beauty of God. It is the same blame-the-victim game practiced by the general society with the added shame of being told you are being ungodly added for good measure.

Every single time a church leader has tried this line on me, they have first behaved in some manner which they would never approve from another person. Often leaning on their very claims of special status as representatives of the truth, they have belittled, betrayed, and/or directly attacked the worth of others. Then, they retreat to statements such as, "Everything would be OK if you just kept 'your eyes upon Jesus . . . and the things of earth will grow strangely dim . . .'"[1] Except the things of earth they want ignored are their own harmful behaviors and teachings.

Yes, I call foul. Both positions cannot simultaneously be true. If people are the current presence of God on earth, then the affront they cause is attached to people's knowledge of God. If their behaviors and teachings are simply their own and people are wrong to confuse them with the beauty of God, then they do not have the right to stand up and claim to speak for God. Internal logical consistency is missing and now so am I. People's behavior is their own, including responsibility for whatever harm and separation that behavior brings. The church must take responsibility when it claims that its words and acts represent God. The Bible does not say that when actions cause another to stumble it would be better if the one who stumbled had never been born. The responsibility is clearly placed upon the one who causes the fall.[2]

---

1. Lemmel, "Turn Your Eyes," refrain.
2. Matthew 18:6.

15

Problem with Teachings on Hell

I have watched with some interest the debates about *Love Wins*[1] and *Erasing Hell*.[2] I only have some interest because I often suspect these *my side vs. your side* books are moneymakers for both people while changing little in what anyone believes or in how we act. Nevertheless, I do find presentations of opposite ways to interpret the Bible interesting.

The concern I have as I write this might be considered practical theology. My issue here is more about the practical effects of beliefs than arguments concerning the interpretation of ancient texts.

I should say up front that evaluating a belief based on how it causes or allows people to act is a questionable practice. People behaving irrationally because of their interpretation of a scientific fact do not change the fact. People misusing a truth revealed by God would not cancel the truth of a revelation. However, a part of *Love Wins* that I think opponents fail to take seriously is that those who do not believe the doctrine will certainly evaluate it by the actions of those who do. The behavior of the believer is the other person's observable reality. I wonder what kind of behavior in this life is tied to the doctrine of hell. I see many offensive acts and messages by Christians telling people that they are going to hell, and I do not see many people attracted to Christianity in the process. I know that I have been offended on more than one occasion by street preachers proclaiming that

1. Bell, *Love Wins*.
2. Chan, *Erasing Hell*.

everyone present was on the way to hell even when I belonged to churches very similar to the ones they wanted people to join.

My central concern is internal to the family of faith. How has the doctrine of hell caused people to behave? I could make an argument that it should cause revolutionary changes in dealing with people seen as *others*. If those *others* are seen as doomed to eternal punishment, any act leading to their death seems evil to me. If our national enemies are among those who do not believe, how dare we wage war and remove forever their chance to be saved? If the criminal is heading to hell, how do we dare to play God through capital punishment and terminate any opportunity for repentance? But, I do not believe this line of thinking is what the world has seen.

I believe that the doctrine of hell has allowed us to harden our hearts. Rather than a deep compassion for those who the doctrine says are doomed, I believe the belief that God condemns people has been translated to our permission to damn people as well. When the aboriginal people of the Americas were labeled as savages beyond the circle of grace, it allowed a callous attitude allowing the United States to commit war[3] against them so that God could reward us, the blessed, with their land from sea to sea. Some did indeed go out as missionaries demonstrating a concern for the well-being of the other. Their work is not to be forgotten even though it also had deadly results in some cases due to the lack of knowledge of disease and medicine at that time in history. But, they were exceptions to national policy rather than examples and also often taught natives that they must accept the destruction of their own culture along with accepting the God of the Bible.

I suspect the conviction that Muslims are bound for hell makes it easier to accept our nation's apparently endless war against them. We are told daily that their belief in our damnation allows their attacks upon us. But, the reflection of the same beliefs in Christianity is seldom considered. I can see how a belief in hell makes it easier to condemn a felon to death when our underlying attitude is that surely God condemns them for what they have done. And it goes further. When those who are supposed to proclaim the gospel of good news cling to verses calling a group of people abominations, does it not numb them to abuse of that group? Even the softer *love the sinner and hate the sin* approach implies that members of the LGBTQ community are welcome in the family of grace only if they cease to

---

3. Genocide is the more appropriate term when we are not trying to justify our own actions.

be who and what they are. Otherwise there are those verses, the ones from the ancient law we choose to remember as opposed to the ones about our own lives which we choose to ignore.

What treatment by man to man is outside the realm of possibility once one adopts a belief that God condemns another person or group to eternal punishment? I remember being taught as a child that black skin was the mark of Cain. God had already marked those that our society abused; never considering that the purpose of the mark was to protect Cain.[4] We know that many Nazis were also church people.[5] If God hated the *killers of Jesus*, why should Europeans not hate the Jew as well? I already mentioned the American expansion. How many mourned the death of pagan natives when God was willing the gift of the land to the Christian nation? If the faithful believe that homosexuality is a chosen lifestyle that will end in condemnation to hell, what measures are too extreme to prevent the corruption of more people, especially impressionable youth? I could go on, but anyone who wants to see will already see and anyone who does not will be growing more offended.

What I am contemplating as I write this is not the truth of the doctrines. Whatever is true about the time after death is true regardless of how we respond to it. I am concerned about the attitudes and actions we adopt based on our beliefs. I would like to consider the alternative of accepting that the heaven and hell we can observe are here. Nonbelievers as well as people of faith can readily identify experiences accurately described by the words heaven and hell in this life, in the present tense. The experiences of life are one's own and do not require arguments from anyone else. We can choose to make other people's lives more heavenly or hellish now in the life we know. It troubles me when a belief in heaven and hell causes people to make others' lives hellish rather than blessed.

Whether we believe in heaven and/or hell is a matter of faith, of trusting certain writings and the doctrines of certain faiths. Neither can be proven in objective terms convincing to those who do not accept the texts and doctrines on which the beliefs are based. My thoughts here are not about whether eternal bliss and damnation are real. They are about how we should live now. There is danger attached to the belief in hell and a God who condemns people to it. Giving in to that danger allows humans to make the lives of other humans miserable. And if those beliefs are correct,

---

4. Genesis 4:15.
5. To be fair, the resistance was also filled with people of faith.

those behaviors can help condemn people to eternal suffering by making faith unattractive. Many of the acts I witness by people of my own early faith now make identifying as part of that tradition unappealing to me.

I wish that those who believe in hell would show more concern for guaranteeing that nobody is forced to live in hell now. I wish that those who believe would be more likely to choose peace than war. I wish that those who believe the stakes are eternal would reexamine anything that causes them to block the door to anyone. I believe practices that bring heaven to as many people as possible now would invite far more to consider its possibility beyond the grave. I believe a life lived in such a way that other lives are made better instead of more miserable is a life correctly lived no matter what happens beyond the grave. We must be careful of the hidden ways our beliefs cause us to adopt attitudes and behaviors which contradict those very beliefs.

16

The Problem of Heaven

Some will wonder what could possibly be wrong with reassuring people with teachings about the wonders of a future heaven. When faced with the loss of people we love, we want it to be true. Promises of future reunions in a place beyond all tears are comforting when all we can do is weep.

However, we know the history of whole groups of people told to endure lives of unjust suffering because there would be reward in the next. Many a child knows the pain of being told that God needed Mom or Dad in heaven worse than they needed them here on earth. And, those of us who care deeply about what we are doing to the planet are appalled by the idea that it doesn't matter because there is a magic new world coming.

Simply put, the largest problem with the doctrine of heaven is that it is focused on out there and some day. We live now and here. If your boot is on my back here, it is not made lighter by your assurance that it will be OK later. The young child needs their loved one with real arms of flesh and blood to lift and hold them here and now. And there is no evidence of a new home we can all move to from this one after destroying our own even though Elon Musk claims the technology he is developing will be able to do it for a rich and powerful few.[1] If it becomes possible, finding and moving on to the next life-sustaining planet after using up our own would make us the villains of all the space invader movies of my childhood. Destroying the only home we have while believing that magic power is simply going to gift

---

1. Mosher, *Elon Musk*.

us a new one, like an over-indulgent parent who replaces each broken toy, is illogical and inconsistent with much of Christian theology.

How many young people have been sent to kill and die with the promise that they will be received instantly into a land of eternal bliss, accompanied or not by a crew of virgins? Is there any greater twisting of doctrines of life than to encourage killing with a promise of instant heaven because you killed on behalf of the right creed or placed your faith in a Jesus who taught his followers to love their enemies? How can heaven await those who are convinced to dedicate themselves to create hell in the only world we know? None of these make sense to me.

Bob Marley cautioned about those who teach that life should be focused on future divine intervention as he encouraged his listeners to fight for their rights now and work for better life here on earth.[2] I know that there are many within Christianity who have taught that working for a more heavenly world here is what the Bible calls them to do. I respect their work. It is not the tradition many of us were raised in or which appears to guide evangelical leaders influencing recent political leaders. Some evangelical Christians ignore all evidence of global warming out of the same rejection of science which has existed since the backlash against the theory of evolution. There are also suggestions that others believe increasing damage to the earth is good. Reading biblical lists of horrible conditions on earth which they believe will precede the return of Jesus, some Christians have decided that destroying the environment and allowing the increase of famine and war are acts that will speed the advent of a new heaven on earth. They do so even though other varieties of their own religion teach completely different interpretations of the same passages.

The ancient Jewish texts however emphasize life here on earth. The human life well lived is one of caring for others and for the earth. The rewards of life are found in this life. Human behaviors are seen in terms of the effect they will have on future generations. The same creation texts read by others now to say the planet was given to man for his willful use and domination are read by other traditions as asserting that man's role has always been as a caretaker for the earth.[3] Simple logic calls for growing knowledge of earth and human interdependence with it to increase caution about how our choices damage natural processes. Altering these views to emphasize that we belong to another home while we simply travel through this life

2. Marley, "Get Up, Stand Up."
3. Genesis 2:15.

destined for that other place, allows also developing ideas destructive to our very existence.

All of this falls within the context of the previous essay on teachings of hell. Non-universalist teachings about heaven lead to identifying those favored of God who will inherit paradise and others who will be banished to its opposite. The doctrine of empire based on the idea that God had chosen Christian Europe for blessings and the rest of the world for damnation is well documented, including its devastating effects on the populations of the lands discovered and claimed by Christian explorers.

I hope there is a heaven. I hope we all end up there in joyous reunion and eternal celebration with all of humanity's diversity present. It is a beautiful dream. In times of deep loss, it is a great comfort. But, all observable evidence tells me that we are of this place and this time. Scientific examination of what we can know shows that when we die our matter and energy return to the unified field of the universe to become part of what remains and what comes to be. This leads me to advocate for a unified field theology. We know what it looks like to create heavenly or hellish experiences for others here. We can strive to make the right choices and live in the correct way based on those observations of what is.

17

Society, Violence, and Religion

Another painful day has come as yet one more person has chosen to open fire on another US campus taking the lives of people who were just attending class. Young people are now taking the lead in pointing out that it is not enough to mourn, express sympathy, and call for new laws while others argue back that more control of our lives is not the answer.

What we will not do is examine the total nature of our society. We will morbidly obsess about the incident and the causes that make no sense. But we will not look into the mirror of violence that pervades our society. Our nation was born in violence—violence to those who already lived here most of all, but also violence between nations competing for new land and resources. During the term of our very first president it was made clear that rebellion at home would be met with force as Washington went in person to put down Shay's Rebellion. We have never altered course.

Citizens are guided to behave, not because of a high national character, but because of ever-expanding laws and a growth industry of prisons. Minorities crying out about disproportionate numbers injured or killed by police are met with majority derision and statements that a sensible person knows to behave and keep your mouth shut in a world where power has the right to kill you. Our response to horrible situations all over the world is that our military should go and destroy whoever we identify as the wrong side. We are part of a national and world order based on violence and the threat of violence.

It goes much further. The very discourse of our leaders is filled with violence. The other party is not merely pursuing policies with which the speaker disagrees. They are trying to destroy the fabric of society, attacking the family, trying to become dictators and offending God. A candidate for president warns that the limitations on free speech he attributes to the other side could allow a Hitler to arise in America. At the same time, members of his own party name the groups of people supposedly responsible for our social and economic ills and entertain discussion of removing them from our soil. It is no longer enough to withhold support of another member's bill if they do not agree with you on an issue. Threats to shut down the government are repeated with each new hot-button issue. Lest that sound like a criticism of only one side, the key word is *threat*. The threats come equally from each side. If we do not win, we will make you pay. This is violence.

It extends even to the way we treat the young. Children are raised into our culture largely through the institution of schooling. And, the pervasive culture of US education is coercive and punitive. The government uses policies of accountability based on threats of removal of school funding and individual employment for failing to meet exam requirements set far from the classroom and the needs of individual students. Everyone will achieve the same levels of understanding on the same material at the same rate or people will be punished. As a result, children are placed under levels of stress leading to documented health problems. But, the culture of education was violent before the current reform era. Physical punishment was once common place for students who committed any act that disrupted the educational process. Grades are used not only to communicate levels of quality and areas for improvement, but as a means to control students and force compliance with whatever requirements we choose to place on the classroom and curriculum. And those who persist in disrupting our norms are simply removed from the school entirely. All of this is well documented by even the friendly critics of education.[1] My point here is simply that even the way we deal with our children is steeped in violence. The effects on children are obvious enough that one would expect parents to demand change. But they do not.

Parents do not rebel about the treatment of their children and those who serve their children as they do not challenge their own treatment at work. Corporations make it clear that they reserve the right to terminate employment of anyone who does not match their company line, or who

---

1. Gold and Mann, *Expelled to a Friendlier Place*.

believes they deserve a fair return for their labor. Union recruitment in the name of protecting people is also coercive. Their very power to protect was won through years of confrontation and violence. The woman who is subjected to workplace harassment often decides that the price of complaint will be too high. The employee who strongly disagrees with the actions of the company knows to save it for the bar and to be very careful about who is present. The norms are clear; stay the course or suffer the consequences.

We depend on coercion—the threat of physical, economic and/or emotional violence—to maintain the order of our society. We do not encourage people so much to achieve their higher selves as to avoid loss of freedom, livelihood, social standing or life itself. We do it at all levels.

I wish I could say that the faith communities of my tradition provided the light in the tunnel. These groups would be a logical place to expect teachings based on becoming better because a higher way exists and can be attained. Sadly, what I have most often encountered is not invitation based on divine love but coercion based on divine and social punishment: accept the love of God or you will be tormented for eternity. People who act outside the rules bring shame to their families and risk exclusion from the community of faith.

Wrapping even claims of divine love in threats of unending destruction, the church itself coerces behavior within a veneer of propriety. Who dares to measure the violence done by cultures that ensure that even attending a place of worship requires pretending that one is alright, on track, straight, in agreement with whatever is preached from the pulpit, and always happy? There are churches that do not work on this basis. So, I have been told. But, my own experience is that in the friendliest appearing churches the threat is there just under the surface—be like us or we will reject you.

And then it happens, again. The young person who believes the rhetoric that blacks are to blame opens fire in a church. The person who believes that abortion is murder decides to kill the murderer as a moral act. The offended driver chooses lethal force to prove their right to the road. Police who are fed up by threats to themselves and constant disrespect justify their own violence as upholding the law. The person who has mentally passed some invisible human boundary decides it is desirable to gain fame or revenge by opening fire on people in class or watching a movie.

And we are all shocked, again. We sit and shake our heads about how *they*, those few, those deranged, those *gun nuts*, those *others* can cause such pain.

Then we go back to work and hold the threat of the performance review over our coworker, to school with the possibility of low scores over the student, to share the *good news* with the threat of eternal hell, and to our homes wielding the threat of filing a complaint on any neighbors who drive too fast or fail to clean up after their dog. We do not think about it. We are numb to the idea that we are the problem. To criticize the system is wrong and dangerous.

What if the extreme cases that bring us all to grief are exaggerated mirrors showing us all too clearly the violence we have learned to tolerate every day as we seek to maintain order in the midst of our lack of unity?

18

Competing Worldviews

I often think US Christianity focuses on the wrong things and presents the wrong face to the world. Many issues are simple questions of whether the views being supported match what the Christian Bible says. These thoughts are about something deeper.

How long will US Christians battle against science? I know it is hard for the person raised on what they believe is accurate literal interpretation of the Bible to accept science that does not match a one-week creation. But, it is not hard for the person raised on science to give credit to an ancient text that gives a surprisingly parallel view of the biological order in which various forms of life appeared on earth. Literal creation and a young earth are alienating arguments designed to allow the person who already believes to keep one certain way of interpreting the Bible. It is not the most serious issue that Christians could spend their time trying to resolve. The same goes for other issues of science—I do not understand how basing conclusions about global warming on observable data is an activity that should challenge religious faith in any way.

The Western church also spends a great deal of energy focusing on issues of the greater society. At times faith has given energy to those who respond to serious social issues by successfully fighting for justice and a more open social order. But, now the news is filled with Christians fighting to protect their narrow views and the right to reject people they disagree with based on doctrine. I can easily see how a person might be offended by being forced to feed or provide a product to people doing something they believe is wrong. But, does defending one's own right to feel good and holy reach out to others? Does it convince anyone else that a view is true or loving? There are more serious issues at stake than protecting one's own feelings.

It seems to me that the most serious issues of Christianity are internal. Christianity as presented by evangelical fundamentalists asks the nonbeliever to accept a God that is frankly hard to accept.

God, knowing everything in advance, creates a world and sets up a situation where man will fail and thousands of years of suffering on earth will occur. But that suffering is man's fault for sin and God is good and just because of promises that it will all be resolved in the end, even though this perfect God created the world knowing the results in advance. That is a hard God to accept even if this life is all that is at stake.

The Bible is presented as the one and only Word of God for all of mankind, even though most human beings throughout history were excluded from knowledge of this book or its God. This God provides a way to salvation by dying on a Roman cross. But, in many US presentations of Christianity, only those who accept this specific salvation are saved and the rest of humanity is condemned not just in this life but to eternal suffering. That is a hard God to accept for a modern nonbeliever not raised within the tradition.

I cannot imagine how it must appear to those from outside the Mediterranean and European areas, places which have lived for millennia outside any knowledge of this plan to save the world. They are supposed to be drawn to faith in a God who provides escape from the trap that God created with full knowledge of the outcome; however, escape is only for the light-skinned people of a small area of the planet for most of world history. That is an issue worth wrestling to the mat in ways beyond simple platitudes about God's ways differing from our ways.

Any parent who placed an innocent child in a setting where they knew the child would behave in ways that led to lifelong suffering would be properly condemned by society and probably imprisoned. Yet, people are supposed to be drawn to a God who does the same. What about parents who provided a path to well-being and happiness then kept it secret from most of their children? But, people are supposed to accept that same type of exclusivity is just and loving when done by God.

In this set of thoughts, I will only give passing mention to the fact that these beliefs have also been used to justify a long list of behaviors by its believers which very few would try to defend today. Among these are

Unified Field Theology

slavery, imperialism, concern for present profit over the health of the earth itself and even genocide. Currently, as mentioned above, it is being used to justify denial of equal rights to people that some Christians believe are living unholy lives. How does that convince the person outside the faith that this God is truly just and that their difficulty accepting the church's teaching on good and evil are only the sinners' perceptions—that it does work out correctly in spite of seeming unfair?

I have spent my whole life inside the circle of US Christianity. I have studied theology across the spectrums of conservative to liberal and ancient to modern. I am ordained and continue to work within the family of faith. But the questions I am presenting are becoming more, not less, troubling to me as time passes.

I do not believe we have adequately answered those who ask how the God we present can possibly be good or just, let alone loving, if that God created the world knowing that the design would result in eternal suffering for most of mankind.

I do not believe that we have sufficiently explained why a just and loving God would reveal the way to live, now and for eternity, to only one very small segment of humanity.

I do not believe we have developed a convincing argument for how a just and loving God would condemn those who do not know the path to holiness to eternal punishment for being born in the wrong places or to the wrong families, or even that love and justice would condemn those thinking people who do not agree that this view of reality can be true.

I seriously believe the issues that the world of faith needs to work on with the most resolve are internal. The doctrines of the faith itself have questions so large and so unbelievable to thinking minds and caring hearts that they deserve better answers than have been given to date.

But, I suppose it is easier and safer to focus on other issues and never confront these questions ourselves.

To be fair, the conservative evangelical narrative is not the most common interpretation of the Bible today or in history, even though it presents itself as the only truth. Mainline denominations and progressive Christians read the same texts with far different lenses and I have learned much from Jewish scholarship on the Jewish portions of the text. A far different narrative is possible that respects what is good and explains why these texts have been kept and treasured for millennia. Those simply are not the story I thought was mine. And they still have problems of internal logic that often reduce to claims that these beliefs are correct because they belong to *us* while insisting that they are universal truth given from beyond the natural world.

I now believe it is possible to begin from within the world we know *is* and build systems of belief and behavior. This system is based on observable reality without resorting to magic guidance from beyond. And, many of the beloved ancient texts from across traditions fit with it in beautiful ways when read through new lenses. There is a path available to a more unifying theology as we examine scientific work and discoveries in search for a unified theory of everything.

19

Christianity Is Not Jesus

Islam is not Allah; Buddhism is not Buddha; Judaism is not Jehovah; science is not Newton, Darwin, or Einstein; communism is not Marx, Lennon or Mao; and United States' democracy is not Washington or Jefferson. As I contemplate these statements, it feels like they should be obvious. No belief system is logically the exact same as its author, its major figure, or its own object. However, as I contemplate beliefs and actions in the emerging twenty-first century, it seems that we often behave as if they are.

My own background in religion is Christianity. In science, my training is post-Einstein, and my governmental exposure has been to US democracy. So, my observations come from within those contexts and interactions mostly with others inside or impacted by the same systems. Many Christians behave as if any questioning of their religious teachings and practices are attacks upon Jesus. Pleased with the predictable universe of Newton, but offended by their interpretations of Darwin and confused by the universe revealed by Einstein, the more fundamentalist wing of Christianity now rejects ideas it does not like by refusing to believe truth revealed by science. Discussions of social possibilities to provide for the general welfare of all citizens, are countered by references to communism and the abuses and crimes committed by the leaders of our Cold War enemies. Any debunking of the myths of the founding fathers raises suspicions of animosity to democracy itself. World news has included many instances of adherents to Islam attacking anyone they believe has disrespected the prophet, and by extension, Allah. This leads me to believe that the problem I am examining extends well beyond Christianity, but I will limit this discussion to my own culture.

Perhaps, an ability to separate paradigms from their authors or sacred objects could liberate us for fuller conversation, greater understanding and human unity, and decreased violence. I wonder if Christians would be more willing to consider the effect of current beliefs and actions in the world if they did not associate all questions with attacks on all that is held holy. I wonder if voters would be more willing to consider humanitarian proposals designed to care for all citizens if they did not immediately associate such plans with Stalin or Mao. I wonder if conservative Christians would be more accepting of the overwhelming evidence of a warming planet if they had not turned their collective backs on the writings of Charles Darwin.

There is much to be gained by a willingness among those who claim to love truth to actually examine and accept factual evidence without prejudice based on the origin of the facts or possible negative implications for their chosen beliefs. We cannot fully explore and understand the capacity of religion to condone, or even foment, violence while we deny the truth of the crusades, the inquisition, world colonization, and the role of Christianity in the holocaust. An honest examination of its own past might equip Christianity to more constructively examine current beliefs and practices toward other religions, other political parties, other countries, and neighbors who do not behave the way that one's church says they must behave. Carefully confronting how the church in the past has failed to obey Jesus' command to "love your enemies"[1] might open hearts to obey the command more fully in the present toward those who disagree with their teachings. The teachings are not Jesus. The teachings are very human explanations of the religion which claims to be based on his instruction. Current and past results of a belief system could be examined without implying complete rejection of that system, if only we could separate the two. Separating the two might be expedited by studying the history of worldwide Christianity leading to understanding that the teachings of the church are not the same across the years, across continents, or even within particular churches over time.

Studying accurate history which separates historic figures from their own myths might allow us to consider that all human governments are associated with human beings and not God given. While I would not go so far as to equate our founding fathers with Stalin or Mao, neither are they free

---

1. Matthew 5:44.

of the sins of slave holding and campaigns of genocide against the original nations of the land we call North America. Careful analysis of US practice over time would show that what we currently practice as democracy has changed in many ways from what the founders originally established and that most of that change has been positive. Perhaps understanding this would lead to greater acceptance of future refinement and improvements for the common welfare.

Allowing a full hearing for post-enlightenment science would require accepting the idea that US literalist interpretations of the Bible are recent, local, and in disagreement with the teachings of the Jewish people who wrote the original texts. If the Bible could be read with greater openness to varieties of interpretation, then science could cease to be considered an enemy of faith.

However, those currently in power in the Unites States have pursued an educational program, now lasting decades, which limits the exploration of fact and interpretation. Educational goals in our society have been narrowed to preparing students to succeed on state-generated tests over specific content delivered in a specific format. Such an education will not prepare students to critically examine the past, present belief and practice, or future possibilities.

The worldview I am proposing in unified field theology requires a broad education considering evidence from a significant variety of sources written in different periods of history. Realizing how current scientific theory and practice came into being requires more than individual worksheets with prescribed question formats. Seeing present culture as one stage in an ever-changing pattern of development requires debunked history which looks fearlessly at who we have been, are, and might become. Letting go of current dogma requires understanding that current beliefs are not eternal, omnipotent, or omnipresent. Neither are current religious leaders omniscient. Those are characteristics of God, not religion.

20

Twenty-First-Century Knowing

Science has reached a level of discovery and theory where the universe can be shown to exist because it exists. The *nothing* before the big bang turns out not be nothing as most people think of it. Before there is a universe there is, in layman's terms, potential. With no things yet in existence, much of what we think of as energy does not exist either. No things are moving. No things are glowing. No things are colliding. But there is potential within what we commonly call nothing.[1]

Then in an instant the condition of the potential is exactly correct and potential becomes actual. Discovery of the Higgs boson and other advancements in physics demonstrate how what is pure potential can suddenly burst forth as existence. First there is energy. Then energy becomes matter. Or put differently, energy packets collect into concentrations that we commonly refer to as matter. But, if we delve down deeply enough, there is energy. It turns out that when we think of light as energy, we produce experiments that show light to be energy. When we think of light as matter, we can design experiments that show it to behave like matter. Our perceptions and our constructions about it change, but light continues to be light.

As the process continues the things, combinations of concentrations of energy, that we know as stars, planets and other space objects form. Then on our own planet, and possibly many others, the energy comes together in exactly the right combinations to become what we know as living matter. Although if everything is examined at the smallest levels, the perpetually

1. Krauss, *Universe from Nothing*.

continuous interactions of energy make that distinction far less than simple observation has led us to believe. We commonly speak of live volcanoes, fire, signals and energy sources. At some foundational level, it all *lives*.

At some point in time our own level of being reached a place where we became capable of energy impulses across nerve connections that we call thinking and contemplation. The combinations that remain stored in our brains become thoughts and memories and we begin the process of trying to explain everything. Having become aware, we assume that everything has meaning if we can only understand it. As creatures that experience pleasure, pain and a final point of perishing, we seek to find meaning in all that is and all that was.[2]

We develop systems of thought (patterns of energy transfer within our brains) that seem consistent with our perceptions. *Good* becomes that which causes pleasure and continued existence. *Evil* is that which causes pain and death. *Inspiring* describes those things that are beyond our explanations and cause us wonder. Thought systems evolve which extend such perception to other things seen as living and life giving. We develop ways of seeing and thinking that allow us to see the death of other living things as good if the energy of that thing can continue the energy which is us.

I now find it very interesting that the ancients wrote down that before there was anything else there was God, the source of all things but not bound by any of the definitions of things or common forms of energy. Able to exist before any *thing*, this ancient term bears odd resemblance to the pure potential now studied by the secular physicist. Then this thing beyond things, speaks—gives expression, manifests in a new way, breaks continuity with pure potential—and the observable universe begins. First there is light, then form, then life. When one resists the urge to apply very recent understandings of human thought and disciplines such as history, along with the urge to turn what was *no thing* into a human form, the ancient myth matches intriguingly with scientific discoveries being made in the search for the theory of everything, or the unified field. Pure potential reaches a point where potential gives birth to everything and time begins.

But energy, and manifestations of energy, do not always behave in ways that favor other arrangements of energy including those we know as ourselves. Lightning strikes; fire burns; predators kill and consume; and human bodies cease to contain the energy we call life for no reason we can observe. And, we want to make sense of it all. We become a species

2. Carroll, *Big Picture*.

that constantly looks backward. All our interactions and our perceptions of them are behind us in time so we really have no choice in the matter. We continue to express stories and explanations of why the universe behaves in the way that it does. Some are ancient and based on beliefs in revealed truth. New explanations based on observable truth and mathematical calculations emerge constantly and point increasingly to unity where older traditions led to separation and violence.

21

Surrender to What Is: I Am

As I continue to think about life and the things I grew up believing, I have recently focused on my relationship to what is. It is easy when I like what is, and too often a source of great emotional disturbance when I disagree with what is.

Eastern philosophy tells me that peace is achieved by learning to set aside self and desires. By letting go of ideas that my thoughts should have power over the world, or that what I desire should happen instead of what is observed, I can live in harmony.

Yet, much of my training emphasizes that what *is*, is wrong. What *is* represents a broken world, a world the church is to work to mend in the present but which will someday be replaced by a new and perfect world. These teachings can lead to great altruism and the alleviation of pain. I would never say that the church should cease from being there when disaster strikes and people are in need. But, there are two sides to the coin. These teachings also lead to a great unease with the world we actually inhabit. There is a constant longing for something other and better.

I have heard many people say that the link between different teachings is love. Beliefs across the world emphasize caring for others as a basic ingredient of the proper life. When I long for a world different from the one we have, I wish this was true. However, those same groups often change to hatred, even destruction, of others when threatened. Believing themselves to be the sole possessors of truth or the favor of heaven, they turn and support violence in word and action against those who are not included.

Love itself becomes a *should* that fails to match what *is*. Relatives, friends and even society fall short of our expectations for what love should be. What is described as our common source of belonging and happiness becomes another source of pain as the world fails to show the concern for our wellbeing that we are taught to expect. It *should* be another way. It is not.

But, I have been contemplating another link in the teachings. Theology, particularly Catholic theology, has sometimes placed emphasis on the *fiat*. The *fiat* is a statement to let something *be*.

The universe begins with Creator's statement of fiat and light. "Let there be"[1] and the universe begins.

The beautiful story of the divine becoming human begins with another fiat as Mary says, "Let it be"[2] as the messenger has told her.

The story of restoring the human and divine relationship comes to a climax in a garden of agony when Jesus submits and issues the fiat of laying down his own will and says of what is going to happen, "Let it be."[3]

And slowly I have begun to suspect that I have been missing something during many years of waiting for something better. There is an emphasis throughout the writings now known as the Bible on what *is*.

In the accounts of Moses, God is pressed to reveal the divine name. I have known the response most of my life: "I am."[4] When the ultimate is pressed to self-identify, the response is "I am." And it begins to dawn on me that the first-person statement of *what is* in correct English grammar is, *I am*.

Perhaps this contains the path to wholeness, to healthy living in the world. The universe pressed to reveal to us how we should respond to it and live within it replies, *I am*. This resonates with other teachings from the East. Wisdom comes when we learn to align with what is, not what might be or should be. I do not believe that it is a mistake that the story of the power of what is contains these fiats. Mary is Mary in the story because she submits to the declaration of what is happening. The story of disobedience from Genesis based on selfish desire to know things like gods and decide things for ourselves is reversed in the statement of the God-man to let it be as God wills as he prepares for death.

1. Genesis 1:3.
2. Luke 1:38.
3. Luke 22:42.
4. Exodus 3:14.

Unified Field Theology

I wonder what level of peace is to be gained by fully accepting the universe that says to us, *I am*. How much of our discontent and pain are caused by insisting on a world that might be, should be or will be? Marcus Borg writes,

> The question of God's existence is no longer about whether there is another being in addition to the universe. Rather the question becomes: What is "is-ness"? What is "what is"? What is reality? Is it simply the space-time world of matter and energy as disclosed by ordinary sense perception and contemporary science? Or is it suffused by a "more," a radiant and glorious more?[5]

My own contention is that the glorious more is indeed part of the universe which science has begun to reveal. I believe that there is evidence within the realm of our observations to assert that the universe and the background field from which it sprang are sufficient to respond to our questions of what is, "I am."

My counter thought is to question whether we must surrender the good that is done in the name of healing the world to accept what is. Must we accept suffering and coldly let it continue to practice a life of accepting that what is, is? I think not.

It seems to me that what we will accept is that nature acts like nature and that death, illness, hunger and need for shelter are real. We may surrender the pain of magic thinking that says we have some power to make the natural world something different from what it is. But when the storm subsides and we have resources to share, that becomes what *is*—people with needs and people with resources. We do not rebel against reality when we share that help. We rebel against reality when we obsess about how it should not have happened and should not be. Taking care of each other is a sharing of the blessings that exist within a world of storms.

I have not fully surrendered. Negative political campaigns make me scream about what should and should not be. So do daily life and watching children struggle to move into adulthood. Illness and suffering of friends make me want to cling to ideas of a magic ability to change the world.

But, I am working toward at least a truce as I admit that none of my desiring alters the course of the universe. The things I like and the things I do not both *are*. I am moving toward a condition of focusing on how we live in peace with what is by caring about each other in the world that *is*.

---

5. Borg, *Convictions*, 45.

That includes accepting that I cannot force others to care. Their journeys, experiences, and responses are theirs and not mine. As difficult as this is, I slowly realize that none of my negative reactions change reality. So, I must do the work of caring about real people, not the images that I would prefer them to be.

It is a long, difficult road. But it seems to me that wise people have been trying to teach us for a very long time that it is less difficult, less disturbed, and less disturbing than trying to deal with imaginary worlds that defy our urging to exist.

The world we inhabit *is*.

The people that surround us *are*.

As I move into the future, I hope to learn more of the joy and peace that come when we dance with reality. This is the path that I describe as unified field theology. We can live, trust, and care for each other within the universe that *is*, the universe that gives us life and accepts back our quanta when our time is finished.

22

I Am: Part Two

Interpreting the text of Exodus 3 so that the name *I Am* applies to the total power of the universe is closely tied to the original text. The narrative continues with miraculous signs and wonders consistent with accounts of power beyond human understanding of the physical realm. Still Moses does not believe that he will be able to convince the children of Israel that he is truly sent as their deliverer and the text says that God is angry with him.

This brings me to another possible interpretation of the text once we step aside from literal reading and allow the text to speak to us in varied, even conflicting ways. According to the narrative, Moses was raised in the house of Pharaoh and educated as an Egyptian; he already witnessed the suffering of his people; and before fleeing to another land he killed one of the oppressors. Now he has lived years in another place raising sheep and learning other ways of life.

If we allow the universe to be sufficient in and of itself within this text, then it is the universe and Moses' own experiences within it that bring him to the point of wrestling with the need to free his people from slavery in a foreign land. Perhaps we can even allow that a man from his tradition and in his time would experience that moment of moral dilemma as visions and conversations with a God. It is easy to see in the narrative that Moses makes no argument about the condition of his people or their need for a deliverer. He knows this. His fear is that the people will not recognize him as that leader. He continually questions who he can say sent him—how he will establish his authority to speak. And he asks for a name.

Each person willing to examine life as part of a natural world, with no power outside of observable reality determining the action and actors, must face this issue. When faced with the need for change, situations where others may not agree with our observations of the world or calls to action, we need an answer for doubts about our authority to speak or act. Moses asks for the identity that gives him authority to declare to slaves that the moment for freedom has come. The answer is, *I am*.

Consider reading this passage without requiring belief that this is literally the cosmos speaking for itself, not the anthropomorphized universe saying that it is sending him. If we refuse to add magic to the stories of our own lives, we may find that the answer is the same. When it is time to assert what is right, to speak to those who may not wish to hear, to observe what is wrong and to stand; the answer which knowledge of the universe leaves us may indeed be that our authority comes from ourselves. When others question who is assuming the right to call for change, the answer that remains to us is, *I am*.

However, once that point is reached, we may also find that new signs of our power and authority appear beyond what we expect. In the narrative Moses experiences the power to have natural things change form, for the incurable to become whole, and is promised that even larger things will happen. We do not have to take these things literally in order to apply them to ourselves. In fact, taking them literally is what prevents us from applying them to ourselves. We can throw all the sticks we want and they will not become snakes. That does not happen in our observable universe. It is the stuff of ancient tales of power. But, we can feel our own spine straighten and our fear of others diminish. As we examine the world and determine the road we must walk, we gain assurance that we may indeed find future power we did not feel in the past. This is the essence of hope.

In a worldview based on the observable universe, we find that individually and collectively we are responsible for our choices about what we will do, what we will oppose, and what we will call others to do. The source of our authority is our competence to examine life and know what is right. When we are questioned as to who is declaring that one action is correct and another wrong, that now is the time for courageous change, that others should follow us; our honest answer is, *I am*.

WHO SAYS?

So, who is offering these observations, musings, reflections and possibilities? I am. I make no claims that what I share here represents pure truth or the only truth. I do not claim that it is inspired by a deity beyond our natural world in order to enlighten twenty-first-century man. These are things that come from my interaction with the world, scientific explanations, and ancient wisdom texts. I leave whether they have meaning for other individuals or groups entirely up to anyone kind enough to share my world for a while by reading and reflecting with me about a system of belief that works to align with the universe that is.

23

Creating a Space for Truth

As I share my contemplations and consider conversations that could emerge as they are shared with others, I am still confronted with the difficulties of language and previous assumptions of truth already discussed. One of the people that gives me hope of opening opportunities to truly hear each other and to move forward in both understanding and being human is Parker Palmer.

I have often used the ideas of Parker Palmer in my own public school classroom and in teacher training. He speaks to a level of interaction between people and possibilities that resonates deeply with who I am and what I do. And, several years ago I stumbled into a wonderful experience with creating "a space in which the community of truth is practiced."[1]

I was given a classroom set of *A Girl of the Limberlost*[2] at my request. Then, I was assigned to teach state history all year. With first semester's student teacher, we struggled through early Indiana, including the native cultures, the pioneers, and the conflicts leading to the formation of the state. This material is usually enjoyable for fourth graders, but that year the lessons became somewhat tedious. Then in January, I decided to do the book anyway. Perhaps a novel from 1909 would become more real to them than truth reduced to facts and standards.

The children did not want the book to end. As we sat together and they read as I read to them, we entered another time in our home space. We

1. Palmer, *Courage to Teach*, 90.
2. Porter, *Girl of the Limberlost*.

met people with ideas and habits very different from our own. We stepped into beautifully described natural environments of a former time. We entered the realm of human interactions with each other and the natural environment. We were able to share awe, love, fear, regret, pain, and great joy through a fictional text.

As we did this, our fiction brought us into contact with truth that will never be recorded in a textbook of facts. As we responded to it and explored our own reactions together as a group of friends we learned things about ourselves individually and collectively that will never be on a department of education's standards list. And it was good. It was very good.

I hated to come to the end of this adventure myself. But the school switched to days of music practice and performances, fundraiser awards, field trips and guests, another round of state testing, and many other ways to sweep away our precious final days together. Neither the kids nor I had any control over all of that. We chose what happened when we gathered in my room. We chose something larger and more real. We choose the sheer joy of learning together about the world and ourselves.

I taught the required material on famous Hoosiers. The students presented most of the material. We explored whatever space those activities opened for us. But, I believe the winter quarter will remain with them as more than content knowledge. I watched this experience travel with them as they moved on through school and life. I repeated the book for several years with new students who arrived asking, "When are we going to do the book?" What we learned and shared, encountered, and celebrated, became part of them and part of me. They carry this with them as part of themselves; part of their knowledge and understanding of our state, yes; but more, so much more. The experience became part of their character, their early experience with a bigger world done in the safety of a caring community, and as an invitation to see new things where others see nothing at all.

I believe teachers and students can explore larger truths in public school. We did it through fiction, not religion, to dwell in a space with truth which exceeded our expectations every day. We were changed. We were greatly blessed. I am grateful.

24

If Humanity Continues on Paths of Destruction

I had a conversation today that would be depressing to most people about the future of the planet and humanity. The current condition is perilous and the odds of sustaining the lifestyles known in the first world during my lifetime are growing smaller.

If one is invested in a particular view of the world, human beings, and eternity that requires our eventual perfection, redemption, transcendence, or even survival it is very difficult to contemplate or tolerate a possible future which is disastrous to the human species. On the other hand, if one realizes that we are important to ourselves because we are self-aware and *not* because we are central to the universe perhaps a larger view is possible.

I was raised on millennial theology that taught we were approaching the point where history would end as the Creator brought the curtain down on humanity's time on earth. Those who were raptured to heaven would continue in bliss; the rest would suffer eternal doom; and earth itself would be replaced by a new undamaged paradise. We saw this as a positive future—believing we were in the group destined for bliss, a new earth, and heaven. Somehow within the circle of those beliefs it was acceptable that most of humanity could end in suffering because we believed evangelical models that implied we could each reach enough people to be saved and continue the cycle in a geometric progression until the number of the saved was sufficient for a just and loving God to end current existence.

Unified Field Theology

I later learned that others interpreted the same texts and teachings as calling upon those with the truth to practice life in ways which would lead to small communities of bliss now and an eventual world of justice and harmony on earth. Love of Creator, creation, and fellow man would overcome our darker tendencies to kill, destroy, and dominate leading to a time of harmony and abundance. Unfortunately, very little evidence about human existence is encouraging that such a trend is or will happen in reality. Humans consume, take, destroy, and commit atrocities both individually and collectively. The scientific evidence of man's impact on the planet leading into the Anthropocene Era contains small examples of positive impact and a much larger picture of consumption and destruction, not a general rise toward perfection.

What does it mean if we destroy ourselves?

If we are the central players and key focus of the universe, it is unimaginable. Our demise renders everything meaningless. The nihil emerges victorious.[1]

However, if the majesty and the beauty are in the universe as a whole, if the total universe is sufficient in itself and magnificent beyond our understanding, we are but observers with no reason to believe we are the only, and definitely not the most central observers and doers in the total cosmic realm. M-theory can take us all the way to saying the entire universe we are capable of observing may be but one of countless universes, but I will choose to stay with only the one we can examine. All the evidence suggests that we are only one expression of the capacity of that universe on one small watery rock on the side of one spiral galaxy.

If we choose to destroy ourselves, or most of what we have known on our planet, it matters to us because this is where we are and we care about our own lives. However, in the total picture, if our collective existence continues to be self-destructive it matters not at all for the continued nature of the universe itself. Attempting to step outside of the human perspective, removal of a destructive life-form might in fact be an improvement in terms of the general well-being of the cosmos. In less value laden terms, an evolutionary blip that was not in the end sustainable would simply have appeared, developed, and ended by its natural course.

I now find it comforting to realize that we are not so large as we have imagined. The universe will continue to do what the universe does with or

---

1. I use the term nihil as *the nothingness*, the chaos which defies any significance or meaning.

without us. The quanta of energy that are currently expressed as human life on this planet will continue to be part of what works in the universe whether expressed as us or not. We matter to ourselves because we have developed the awareness of self. But, the universe will be fine with or without us.

This causes me to consider the teachings of my youth with a new twist. Perhaps they might be read as warning rather than golden promises for the faithful. There could come a time when the restoration of beauty and magnificence to this small corner of what is would come by our removal. The religious see it as happening at the hand of an external God. Scientific evidence might place it more in the realm of the end of a plague after the epidemic of human existence has run its predictable course. It makes little difference. The totality of the universe will continue functioning in ways which we are beginning to have the capacity to appreciate but which do not require our participation.

If the universe expressed itself in our language, it would continue to say, *I am*, even if we end our participation. I have become aware of my existence as one expression of that larger existence in ways that bring me comfort despite expectations of doom.

25

We Have Our Stories

Human beings are storytellers. From our perspective, this seems to be one of our unique traits. We do not know if the songs of the whales or verbalizations of other species contain story. But, absent understanding, we assume they do not. Humans, however, have been telling stories even before we developed means of recording them. As we remember and reflect on our experiences, look at the world in wonder, or face the fears and possibilities of the future—we form stories. And they matter to us.

One of the many quotes I kept on my office desk says,

> Remember on this one thing, said Badger. The stories people tell have a way of taking care of them. If stories come to you, care for them. And learn to give them away where they are needed. Sometimes a person needs a story more than food to stay alive. That is why we put these stories in each other's memories. This is how people care for themselves.[1]

I find it profound. When we encounter things that do not fit our knowledge or beliefs about the world, we experience cognitive dissonance and seek meaning and understanding. When we are filled with wonder, we seek to communicate the beauty we feel in our experience of awe with others. When we are startled by the fragility of life and the suddenness of death, we seek to comfort one another and we do all of these with story.

---

1. Lopez, *Crow and Weasel*, 60.

Some of our stories are fleeting. We tell them over dinner or to share our day and they live for a moment and pass into the silent past. Some become repeated themes and we know that Grandpa is going to tell that favorite story sometime in every visit. When that person passes, the story may reappear occasionally as a treasured memory of the person and then gradually fade away. Some stories persist while a culture lasts and then disappear as people groups change and cultures are lost.

But some of our stories transcend. Some are too treasured to fade away. They are maintained through generations even among oral cultures. With the advent of writing some are recorded and lost, but others are recorded and guarded, treasured, maintained, and shared across centuries and millennia. These stories give expression to things we cannot explain with direct language. They express the things we treasure most and long for from deep within our collective selves. They express hopes for a world that might be, *if only*. They define who we believe we were, who we are, and who we hope we might become.

It is very much out of respect for this value of shared story that these essays are written with great encouragement from my mentor, Don Pitzer. We live for a short season and the quanta invested in us by the universe moves on to be expressed in new forms. But, the things we write can outlive us. We record them and if others find value in them, they are kept. We express our vision of the universe and we submit it for the review of others. If it resonates with the world they know, or wish we all knew, then the ideas and stories are kept and passed along and a community of thought becomes a reality greater than the musings of a single life. These essays are a humble offering into that tradition.

I confess a lifelong love of the stories so precious that they have survived the millennia. Through times of war and peace, plenty and hardship, the shifting of cultures and the expanse of human knowledge, they persist as guides for both mind and heart. I do not want anyone to take my reflections as evidence that I reject the wisdom passed down to us in the ancient texts or fail to see the beauty in the narrative and its individual parts.

While my mind and heart reject insistence that I take story as fact, and poetry and metaphor as history written long before any discipline called history became reality—my heart clings to the beauty in them. They do not have to be historical facts to be truth. They need not be simple recollections of happenings to be powerful expressions about the traditions and cultures which produced them—as well as criticisms and hopes for the human condition. Considered as story which mattered enough to be recorded and preserved, they are powerful enough to stand alongside science in our libraries. They help us to understand what it means to be human in a cosmos enormous beyond our experience or imagination.

26

Mystical Experiences

Where does a focus on the universe we can know through observation leave us when we experience things beyond our prosaic explanations? What do we do with the stories of those, myself included, who report mystic experiences?

Many of us who love the outdoors have experienced that sort of transcendent belonging that happens sitting by campfires in small groups. Christian upbringing often includes an expectation that by believing the correct things, living in the correct way, or adopting certain forms of prayer one can experience the presence of God. Some of us experience things beyond anything we were taught to expect or accept, experiences that go beyond all our explanations of human experience.

I still remember the overwhelming sense of joy and belonging that came over me leading to my first answer of an alter call to become a Christian at age six.

I have often experienced an instant sense of deep connection when meeting other people for the first time. This has gone so far as to include an awareness of communication between myself and the other person across language barriers with no audible exchange.

I have often experienced Zen-like moments of unity and well-being when climbing the face of a cliff or hiking above timberline in the wilderness of Colorado.

In 2005 I was on a cliff in Ethiopia when I became very dizzy and had the sensation that everything was spinning. Figuring it was mild

Unified Field Theology

dehydration, I took time to drink some water and then tried again. Everything was still spinning and then, for one of the only times in my life, I became convinced that I was not supposed to finish the climb. I had a strong impression that my focus was supposed to be toward home and my family. I returned to a lower level and spent the afternoon there with my wife waiting on the others who climbed to an ancient rock church which I really wanted to see. That evening at the hotel we learned that a tornado had gone through our city, within sight of my home, and had killed over thirty people. The time stamp on our pictures confirmed that the tornado was going past our four daughters at the same time I experienced spinning on the other side of the world.

I have seen things in nature which hyper-focused my attention and brought to my mind awareness of lessons I needed to learn, unhealthy attitudes I needed to let go, or just a sense of peace and wellbeing. More than once this has included experiences that resulted in joyous laughter that I expressed at the time as laughing with God. One day while driving Indiana backroads to reach Indiana University I started noticing turtles crossing the road. They kept showing up in numbers that seemed unusual. Having recently become very stressed about political situations at work, I took it as a sign to slow down and relax. Just as I gave expression to that thought, the car in front of me caught a turtle by the back of its shell and shot it off into the woods. I laughed out loud and said, "OK, God, 'Not too slow or they will run over your ass.'" I had a wonderful laugh with what seemed to be a power greater than myself.

In 2000, I was on the summit of Quandary Peak in Colorado preparing to descend when my vision and legs both failed. I was part of a group of eight people and responsible for helping to make sure everyone was safe. But, my legs had turned to rubber and my vision was too blurry to see as I stood facing a path of loose boulders and snow above 14,000 feet. I remember looking up at the sky and saying, "God, your sense of humor doesn't match mine again!" Then I asked to be able to see just the next step. That is how much my vision cleared, enough to see one step at a time. It was a long and difficult trip down the mountain with a friend and coworker who was also suffering from over exposure. But, it has become a strong metaphor of life that I often remember. Most of the time all we can really see is the next step to take.

So, I must deal with the reality that people have such experiences. Things happen in odd ways and cause reactions in us that are not easily captured in prose or the equations of simple science. Many of us have understood these things to be experiences of, even proof of, God. But, they prove nothing to other people, except possibly that they have reason to doubt our sanity or judgment! I have had some heated conversations with atheists or agnostics who have grown weary of people using their own experiences to try to prove something is universally true. Such personal experiences do not transfer easily to others who have not shared the experience and who do not agree with conclusions made about them. These same conversations became very friendly when personal experience was allowed to remain personal and not used as evidence against the other person's views and beliefs.

While I recognize that the most hardcore materialists would say it is all coincidence and imagination, I believe that such phenomena occur. I find them important and believe there are lessons which one can take from them. However, I no longer believe that they require explanations based on forces beyond the observable universe. New research into the brain is adding to our understanding everyday of how different regions of this amazing organ receive and process nerve impulses. While I will not reduce such happenings to mere imagination, I know that the human mind has an amazing capacity to perceive the world at levels which exceed the simple recording of light and shadow. We also have powerful centers of sense making and storytelling which allow us to respond to what we have seen and felt. I believe there are times when these things happen at levels beyond simple observation, imagination and telling. The person in the midst of them feels something more than the commonplace.

Quantum physics may speak to these issues as well. Carefully replicated experiments have shown that particles seem to communicate across significant amounts of space. Simultaneously fired particles demonstrate opposite spins in spite of careful efforts to eliminate any known connection between the two events. While it is most comfortable to think of our bodies as collections of clearly defined organs which are in turn made of clearly identifiable cells, at the bottom of it all we are made of these quantum particles. In addition, various forms of energy and multitudes of these particles are constantly traveling through and for brief moments of time occupying the same space as our bodies. We have yet to begin to understand the implications of this dance of energy and matter that we simply call our own bodies. Some scientists are even exploring controversial theories that the

Unified Field Theology

universe itself might also be self-aware as the same quanta exist in many forms of varying complexity and in the cosmos considered as a whole.[1]

Realizing that earth contains a set amount of carbon which appears and reappears in the form of various substances and life-forms including us, I have quipped with tongue only partially in cheek on more than one occasion that what occurs at night by a fire involves the communication between carbon atoms. We are composed of them. So is the fuel we burn bringing its carbon to higher and higher levels of energy for our light, warmth, and comfort. We do not know enough to label as total nonsense the idea that there is interaction between the quanta of energy we consider to be our carbon atoms and the carbon atoms we consider separate from us in the fire. Perhaps, some part of our biology is able to respond to quantum interaction at levels beyond our conscious understanding.

At this point one can dance right over the edge of the new age cliff and babble about theories of human soulmates being made of material from the same stars, or claim special knowledge of how alignment of our vibrations brings connection. I am not suggesting that there is any wisdom in taking the path of fantasy for anything except entertainment, especially when someone is skillfully packaging it for financial profit. I love the mystery of things that, as of now, exceed our understanding and ability to quantify and analyze. However, I no longer believe they require explanations that stretch beyond what we know to exist within the universe.

And still, I remain a mystic. In the woods and on the side of a cliff I experience my connection to the biosphere in deep and personal ways. When wonder, or humor, strike me in my encounters with what is, I let them embrace and enfold me. I believe there is much in the universe from the macro discoveries of astrophysics, to the tiny miracles in a small sample of earth or water, that can take the human mind and spirit to transcendent levels of experience. Sharing those experiences directly or in story with others who understand, forms deep bonds of mutual understanding. They fail when stretched to become stories that must be true for others.

I look again to the ancient texts and I see much to indicate my kinship with these earlier generations. I believe they dreamed dreams and saw visions. I have no doubt that they found great meaning in them because they took the effort to record them and others have found them important enough to preserve for millennia. If I enter the text in full participation, I can get a glimpse of Moses on the mountain or early humans gazing with

---

1. Powell, *Is the Universe Conscious?*

both fear and wonder at our world. And I know I share with them a capacity at times to let the experience envelope me in ways that exceed my predictions or vocabulary.

It is OK. We live in the enormous and wonder producing complexity of the universe. I validate my own experiences in it as well as those of each person who chooses to share theirs with me in person or across the centuries. However, I no longer require another person to be ruled by anyone else's perceptions of their own life encounters. The world of the mystic is a beautiful thing to share and a horrible instrument for domination. The mystic in me simply invites the mystic in others to feel the joy and to dance along with the cosmos.

27

Myth

There are high and low views of myth. I grew up with a low view of myth which is commonly found in dictionaries. This view sees myths as ideas or stories that are believed by many people but that are not true. With this understanding of the word, any reference to a person's religious beliefs or texts as myth is an insult. While most people in the United States are comfortable speaking of the stories of Greek Gods as myth, many would be highly offended by referring to the accounts of the Bible in the same way.

What I will refer to as the high definition of myth is also described by *Merriam-Webster* online as:

> 1 *a* : a usually traditional story of ostensibly historical events that serves to unfold part of the world view of a people or explain a practice, belief, or natural phenomenon
>
> 2 *a* : a popular belief or tradition that has grown up around something or someone; *especially* : one embodying the ideals and institutions of a society or segment of society[1]

I encountered this way of viewing myth through the history text *Myth and the American Experience*, by Nicholas Cords and Patrick Gerster. I find it to be a very powerful way to view both the stories and character of people groups. It is not necessary for Parson Weems's famous story of young George Washington and the cherry tree to be literally true in order for it to represent a social desire for US leaders to be honest and trustworthy

---

1. *Merriam-Webster* online, s.v. "myth."

individuals. On a more negative note, stories of minorities as people who are less able to learn and more likely to have undesirable social traits do not have to be true in order for those attitudes to persist over time and drive unfair treatment of those groups. My emphasis here will be on the positive use of myth to express worldviews and ideals. Like the work of fiction which I enjoyed with my students, story often communicates big ideas about abstract concepts more powerfully than simple declarative prose.[2] Likewise, art, music and poetry often convey ideas and feelings in more powerful ways than factual prose. I have included footnotes to songs by a few artists that I believe demonstrate this in their lyrics.

I was raised in a tradition which saw all the stories in the Bible as literally true. Miraculous events happened in ways never recorded since the advent of science and history as modern disciplines. The characters in the stories were all real people who did exactly what the text declares, even to the point of having the exact conversations quoted in the Bible. Any suggestion that these were less than literally true was received as a sign of unbelief or liberal misinterpretation. But, the stories taken literally raise multiple issues. God's favored individuals lie, cheat, steal and even commit murder.[3] Their God does not appear much better. Humankind is created, then God regrets it and kills all but one family and all the animals that can be fit into one large boat. God chooses a favorite people and authorizes them to take possession of the land he is giving them by killing every human being already living there and even their domestic animals. Within the circle of fundamentalist belief, these human behaviors are often presented as proof that God can act through humans in spite of their faults and weaknesses. God is allowed to do anything God wants because it is right by definition when done by God.

Part of my own journey away from this way of thinking came from beginning to read rabbinic literature. What Christians typically call the Old Testament and read with an emphasis on how it leads to the New Testament books of their own faith, consists of the writings of the Jewish tradition with some differences in translation and wording. I decided it would be academically more honest to read what people from within that faith tradition said about their own ancient texts. These readings revealed a beautiful variety of interpretation within the rabbinic tradition. Different rabbis

---

2. Borg, *Convictions*, 105.

3. Claims that the Creator of everything and everybody picks favorites are automatically a problem for me.

often present very different interpretations of the text and truth is allowed to exist in the dynamic of discussion and argument.[4] While there is a very conservative and literal tradition, there is also a rich tradition of reading the texts as powerful myths which reveal not only truths about the past, but instruction and guidance for current behavior as well. I find this tradition far more powerful. Some who remain primarily literalist, may be able to benefit from considering these broader meanings by assuming that a single piece of writing can have multiple layers of meaning. Those who cannot, have probably already abandoned any hope of finding meaning here. For those who can no longer believe stories that resemble Hollywood special effects more closely than anything directly observable, what I am suggesting is an invitation to reexamine these ancient texts as myth, song, poetry and metaphor. Read in these ways, the truths that have caused them to be revered and preserved over millennia may become more available and powerful.

Modern examples can be found in the fiction writings of C. S. Lewis. *The Chronicles of Narnia* and *The Space Trilogy* make no claim to be literally true. They are fiction. And yet Lewis managed to weave into these writings many lessons about human behavior, the meaning of life and faith, and images of his Christian faith. Many of us who love these writings have found that Lewis' descriptions of a magical earth-like place and a powerful but self-sacrificing God in the form of a lion, communicate our heart truths in ways that nonfiction theological essays seldom match. Likewise, many who grew up in very conservative religious traditions continue to find deep meaning in the music and poetry of faith long after literal interpretation of the texts has become impossible to accept.

I invite the reader into this relationship with the ancient texts. There is much to be gained by approaching many of these accounts as stories too true to be mere facts.

---

4. *Hebraic Literature*, translated and edited by Maurice Harris.

28

Dream about Caring Enough to Act

I sometimes wake up from a strange dream with the feeling I am meant to remember it.

In this dream, I was with a large group of young people. All were dark headed and could have been from anywhere in the eastern world. They were seated in neat rows on a hillside and each had a container of food in front of them. Some had containers of liquid. Some had baskets of food. There were hundreds of these children and there was a sense of victory in the scene.

Somehow, I already knew that they had engaged in an act of civil protest to gain food for their area. Now with the food, they needed rides back home and were waiting for trucks to show up from the government to take them home. For a wonderful moment, it was a scene of peace and happy community. Then I experienced the strong sense that a government that had to be prodded into providing something as basic as food to its young might show up with force rather than friendly rides home.

The scene became even more like a movie as I rallied them with the cry that whether this was the day of victory or of their deaths it must be met with dignity. As I called on them to respond all stood and began to sing a song, the song of their movement. They stood and sang watching for what was to come.

But one girl had an instrument, an accordion of all unpleasant things, and was able to play her own song so loudly that the group's song could not be heard. I could not hear and did not know the words. My wife was with us and she knew the song and was singing with the children. But, I could not hear or join the song. So, I took the girl's instrument from her and let her know that I found her behavior rude.

What interested me most came next. I was no longer with the whole crowd but talking with the girl. I was giving back her instrument and advising her to leave. If she was against what was happening, it would be ridiculous for her to risk death by staying. I was even advising her that she might become known as a hero for standing against us if the government came and killed us all. She could be known for a lifetime as the one who stood with her country when it looked like its opponents had won.

Then, I woke up wondering why in the world I had this strange dream and why I thought it mattered.

The first image that came back was of those youngsters singing like Native Americans singing either a song of victory or a death song. These are traditionally the same song. They seemed heroic to me. I agreed with their cause which seemed to me to be one of basic justice. My ignorance of the song made it clear to me that I supported their cause but was not truly one of their group. I was proud of my wife for having become more of an insider than myself.

But as I continued to search for what I was being told, the young woman who opposed us came back to me as the most significant. Like a lesson I already knew, it became apparent to me that in a world where such things were real, I cared deeply about her because she dared to *act* on her beliefs. It was urgently important that she did *something*. Even though her beliefs were different from ours she was also a person committed enough to act. She was committed enough to take actions that made her alone in a crowd of hundreds fully devoted to the opposite view. And I truly wanted the best for her.

Sometimes the crowd is right. Sometimes it is wrong. Sometimes we are called to stand alone. Sometimes standing with the crowd can be a fatal act. But in a world of injustice, every person who dared to move beyond mere thoughts and words to action mattered. And I loved them all.

I hope I can live that. I hope I can value the person or the people who care enough to stand for what they believe, whether they are on my side or not. Giving up the assertion that only one view can be correct at the same time can open us to greater possibility of unity within diversity.

29

How Do We Live?
Problems with Current Models

If we accept a world based on what we know rather than what a particular version of the ancient wisdom literature tells us, how do we live? How do we choose the most appropriate individual and group behaviors without the pronouncements of a higher authority?

I have read other sources that try to establish universally observable human standards of right and wrong. I simply do not find them convincing. Leaving aside the individual who chooses to perform acts outside of group accepted norms, the groups themselves do not consistently obey any list of common rules for behavior. The Golden Rule exists in multiple forms across religious traditions. However, people within those traditions continue to exhibit self-interest, greed, and various forms of violence toward others. Most social groups have pronouncements against murder. But, when diplomacy fails and groups go to war, the killing of others we have never met is both allowed and encouraged by the state. When we are sufficiently offended by the acts of an individual we authorize those who work for the state to kill that individual while they are helpless to defend themselves. Very old finds in anthropology show weapon marks and signs of violence on human bones. It seems that our species tends both to protection and nurture and to injury and destruction of others based on situations, not by universally accepted rules.

From this most basic level of taking the life of another, one can proceed through all levels of behavior. Rape? Some cultures still condone abducting child brides from other villages and forcing them to submit as a matter of culture. Countries under Islamic law continue to allow the blaming and killing of the person who was raped as a matter of honor. Even the text of Deuteronomy only considers rape a crime punishable like other sexual crimes if the woman is already assigned to another man. If she is not pledged to another man, the rapist is simply considered to have married her and must give her family silver and remain married to her for life. There is no mention of her freedom to leave and not continue to be the man's sexual partner.[1]

Most groups claim to have rules against theft. But groups that believe all cattle were created for them approve the taking of cattle. Part of becoming a full warrior in some US native tribes included the stealing of ponies. And, Americans will often voice beliefs that *business is business* in response to situations where one party takes advantage of another through dishonest statements or lack of honesty in transactions.

My own observations of people who claim to live by unquestionable rules given by God in the Bible are also less than convincing. People who claim to believe that sex is reserved only for those who are legally married, frequently marry when they discover that the future wife is pregnant. People who say they believe it is wrong to consume alcohol, consume it at home or special occasions where it would be rude not to accept the refreshments provided by the host. Old jokes abound about Baptist deacons only being allowed to smoke behind the church and people who attend the same church not recognizing each other at the bar or strip club. Recent heat over issues of rights for LGBTQ couples never seemed to upset the religious people of my youth as long as such pairs were identified as a couple of old maids or two confirmed bachelors who happen to live down the street. Now that telling the truth has become common, I see religious people using ancient verses to condemn the behavior of others while ignoring rules from the same texts about shaving, eating shrimp, wearing clothing made of more than one kind of material, or eating pork. When openly discussed, the rules that seem to condemn others are quoted and the ones that apply to one's own life are disregarded. My own conclusion is that most religious rules are about behaviors that are condemned in others, and done in secret by the faithful with the real prohibition being against openly discussing such actions.

---

1. Deuteronomy 22:28.

One of the most widely practiced rules seems to be to maintain a calm appearance of order within one's own group. A talented gay music leader at church is a gift from God as long as their sexuality is never discussed. Pastors may leave their families for a new person they have an affair with as long as they quietly leave the church that knows and set up practice in a new location. Many couples married in a church have their first child in less than the biologically required time with no scandal as long as nobody mentions the fact. The most fundamentalist churches require strict obedience to the rules of their teaching, even when it represents a cruelty—until an infraction occurs that would cause great disruption to the organization if recognized. Then, the game often becomes how to keep everyone quiet and pretend that nothing happened. Order and the preservation of the group appear to be the bottom line in both enforcing and ignoring the publicly claimed rules.

This interests me when compared to the second law of thermodynamics. The direction of the entire observable universe is toward higher entropy. Nature tends toward the lowest energy state with the highest degree of disorder while behavioral teachings for human behavior go to great lengths to maintain order and avoid chaos. Perhaps this is exactly as it should be. In a world that tends toward ever-increasing disorder, humans feel a natural need for systems that maintain order and predictability. On the other hand, it may represent a desire to be outside of and more powerful than the rules that apply to all things; to be gods.

My point and conclusion here is that the ideas I am exploring in considering science and its implications for human life do not violate currently existing universal standards. Simple observation reveals that no such universally accepted standards exist to be violated. In thousands of years of human behavior and contemplation some patterns have emerged. Ideas about proper treatment of other human beings have been formulated and adapted. Yet people, including the groups that claim those ideas and beliefs, have challenged, refused to submit to, and revised those rules. This is especially true when groups feel threatened and seek safety through behaviors which violate their stated beliefs or when enough time passes to erase all memory of the purpose of a belief or practice. My current efforts are merely to continue the process of comparing what we are learning about the world to what we conclude about ourselves.

30

Particle Behavior

I turn now to look at the behavior of particles, because I think the small is the best analogy to man, and of large space objects to see what this new science might offer as guidance for universal behavior.

Much of our knowledge of very small particles, including the relatively large mass Higgs boson, so important to current theories of the nature of the universe, comes from experiments in super colliders. These massive machines generate incredible amounts of energy in order to fire small bits of matter into other matter at very high speeds and cause collisions and explosions that reveal their building blocks. What strikes me as most important about this in contemplating the natural behavior of objects is the amount of effort required to make matter destroy other matter. Our knowledge derives from forcing these tiny bits of matter to act in ways contrary to their normal behavior.

When we look to the skies we see more normal behavior of natural objects. They are drawn together in ways that are most often nondestructive. Gravity draws objects toward each other. But speed and the nature of movement across the space-time continuum cause them to circle each other. Planets orbit stars. Stars form clusters and galaxies that spin around one another. There are black holes that draw matter into themselves in ways theorists are still probing and seeking to explain. Whole galaxies are believed to collide. But, the overwhelming normal is that large objects naturally fall into patterns mimicked when humans dance. It is in the exception that we see destructive collisions.

Particle Behavior

When we turn to the very small, this remains true. Some larger particles like neutrons and protons form tight clusters bound by one of nature's greatest forces. High-speed small particles like electrons occupy layers, jump layers, and can be enticed to travel across atoms producing the electricity upon which the world has come to depend. But, their wild and high-speed travel does not result in the catastrophic collisions that allow us to observe the smaller quanta of the universe. To see those, we must construct massive machinery which forces matter to travel at very unnatural speeds and directions and then record our observations of the aftermath.

Perhaps we should consider this as a pattern or metaphor for human behavior. Social science has long theorized that the evolution of cities and farming are interconnected. Recent discovery of worship sites which predate known cities and farming are causing some to revise the probable order of events and theorize that the desire to worship, or control, forces larger than man may have required the evolution of farming and cities.[1] But maybe, gathering into clusters and tribes is as normal for humans as it is for animal herds, heavenly bodies, and the particle building blocks of nature. When more people are drawn together than can be protected by natural shelter, building collections of shelters is predictable behavior. Whatever caused this collectivity, production of greater quantities of food than hunting and gathering can provide is also a natural step. I am not so concerned by the behavioral chicken and eggs as what we may see as the universal model for how to behave in these collections of people.

I believe it is easy to demonstrate that we are more attracted and more tightly bound to some humans than others. There is a negative racist twist that could be made here with some support in observable behavior of humans over time. But, I believe the attraction has more to do with genetic kinship and similarity in behavior. Some human clusters attract us enough to cause us to orbit for a time and possibly to acquire great energy, but not to become part of the tight inner group.

But, it seems to me that observation of the universe can lead to a logical conclusion that we are not meant to collide with each other or to destroy one another. We have the observed potential to gather in ever more complex combinations that appear for a time and often dissolve again into new groupings and formations. And we normally coexist in ways that are not harmful to others within our clusters or to other constellations of people.

---

1. Curry, "Gobekli Tepe."

Unified Field Theology

We do not yet understand exactly what happens as galaxies collide. We do not know if planets seek new orbits as the gravity of other large objects interferes with the pattern of their own star system. We know that being drawn into proximity to the energy of another star will inevitably create too much heat for planets to continue as they were before. The heat may consume them.

The same seems to me to be true for the collision of large groups of people. Some seek to find new patterns of belonging, in sociology terms they seek to accommodate to the emerging situation or culture. Others resist or are rejected. We know by observation that considerable heat and destruction often occur. But perhaps it is a mistake to see those occasions as any more normal than the rare collision of star systems.

I think there is ground here to choose human behavior based on what will happen in each of our encounters with others. When the new encounter is attractive to us, we may form new attachments. When the new encounter repels us, we may move away, possibly with high speed and energy. But, we do not have to collide. We do not have to destroy. Indeed, those are not the normal example of the cosmos. My current approach to life, my conviction of how I am intended to live, is to pay attention to each interaction as it comes. In each encounter with other humans—and with other living things and forms from nature—I seek to do no harm. My intention in each encounter is to allow the other to be itself without any imperative on my part to react negatively. As a cognitive and reflective being, I can choose to make each encounter positive for the ones I encounter. And I believe it is the model of nature that the encounters at least remain neutral, sometimes attractive, sometimes energizing for movement in different directions, but not to engage in collisions which harm the other. Good dancers do not collide.

And then I turn back to the teachings of the ancients across continents and I hear harmony. The tribal people of the world retain many teachings about living in harmony with all of life and with the planet itself. The wisdom of the East called people to stop striving against what is and to move through the world being present to what is without seeing ourselves as superior. And the lessons of the Bible itself called upon the distant ancients to walk justly and love mercy—to live in nondestructive ways in interactions, especially with the weak. Jesus taught that no goal was higher than love for one's neighbor and for the source of our being. Call it Creator, the Tao, the space-time continuum, or the Higgs field; we all come from that source and return to it. Wise teachers have long sought to guide us to see our brother and sisterhood with all things and to live in harmony with what is.

For me it fits. One does not have to accept only one limited dogma as ultimate truth in order to follow the normal path of the universe. It is natural to draw close and to move away, to collect in tight groups and to move in productive orbits, to form more complex and productive combinations without seeking to destroy the others that draw near us. And it all happens while we are also rushing outward into new space.

Choosing a specific dogma attached to the cluster of our birth as the only truth is shown in the mirror of history to often place us inside the collider. Altering our normal behavior to match our religious, political, or national beliefs, humans have taken the path of collision and destruction. Then when the heat dissipates, we seem to remember that those we sought to destroy are very much like us after all and new patterns and interactions are formed to allow peaceful coexistence and even greater productivity.

I think we now have, and have always had, the choice to live in harmony with what is—to follow our orbits and clusters without denying others to do the same. We do not have to engage in conflict and destruction. In fact the universe itself shows us that such behavior is outside the normal patterns of existence. Perhaps from the distance of Archimedes elusive lever platform, we would even gain the clarity to see we aren't that different anyway as we are all made of the same particles and move by the same natural laws. This opens the door for a new unified field theology.

31

The Gravity of Nothing

The light beam that inspired these musings is the quasar. The quasar is the brightest light known to man and it comes from the center of a black hole absorbing more than it can contain. I am thinking about the phenomenon in physical images, but primarily in relation to the meaning we try to deduce.

Current black hole theory says they are extreme amounts of mass concentrated in the smallest possible space. Scientists are starting to get actual images of the event horizon surrounding the Milky Way's central black hole. The size of the stars in the pictures versus the event horizon seem to show a very large dark space. What if it is the space, not just this dense spot in the middle, which is drawing in the surrounding matter?

What if the strongest gravity, the strongest attraction force, in the universe is what we have always called nothing? What if the same nothing from which all things come actually draws them back again? Such an action would parallel observed natural functions like earth's water cycle. The waters rise, fall, and flow back to their origin in continuous cycle. If the background of the universe itself calls all things back to itself, it would show that what we call the circle of life applies far beyond earth's biology. Things *live* and then they return to their source.

Think about simple physics with vacuums. To try and create one, we need a very strong bell jar and a strong seal. We are told that the inward pressure is due to the weight of air in the atmosphere. But, what if the simple and naive interpretation also contains truth? Just like gas released into a room, molecules which move freely do *not* drop to the earth, they spread to fill the greatest possible amount of space. Both the molecules released in an empty room and the ones surrounding a space we artificially try to empty move to what we see as emptiness.

Gravity works better on liquids, but given time even they tend to escape as gas and move out into the emptiness rather than remain concentrated in our bowls. Thinking about very old buildings and mountains themselves, they also disappear back into the energy field and cease to remain as physical realities. We have all kinds of explanations of how this happens from various fields of science, but things return to non-things given the proper amount of time.

Why do large space objects orbit? I have read the most complicated explanations from the combination of inertia and gravity to the shape of the space-time fabric being stretched or warped near large objects. What if comets, planets, stars and galaxies are drawn not just to each other but to the emptiness as well and orbits are their most elegant balance?

What if the background *something* that exists where there is *no thing*, also draws all things to itself? These ideas could relate to the search for the illusive dark matter and energy, but mostly they are my own philosophical musing rather than scientific observation.

It makes both physical and spiritual sense to me. Meditation is most powerful when there is no goal, no seeking of enlightenment or wisdom— just a letting go to be part of it all again. I could almost feel it physically while imagining all of this. My body is but a temporary sack of fluid riding through an amazing universe composed of things that appear to be real but which really are energy concentrated in limited spaces for brief periods then returned to the background field again. It makes sense to me, in observable quasars and in the different theories on how black holes may work, that huge amounts of what existed for a time rushing back into the source would allow us to "see a great light!"[1]

One of the places I have clung to Christian ideas of heaven and even to the Second Coming is in regards to death and grief. I have said on more than one occasion, "I pray for the day the King is here and we no longer have to suffer being left behind when a loved one is called home." And I have usually declared it through tears that came against my will. And then I think of an idea which appears in more than one religion, that we can die to self now and yet continue living. Siddhartha doesn't have to leave

1. Matthew 4:16.

immediately for Nirvana, rejecting separation from all that is and isn't, he can choose to stay and help others. The *power in the blood* isn't magic in bodily fluid, it is power in the willingness to surrender even human existence and return to the source, the Creator, showing us the way.

As a non-physicist, just a joyrider on Einstein's beam, I think there could be a path to unified theory in this. If whatever the background source is has its own attraction force or gravity, maybe gravity does fit with the rest of the forces—we just get confused because we believe there must be an object for there to be gravity. In basic physics, we talk about energy as exhibited on or by objects, but we know now that it can travel through or across what we call emptiness.

And it makes a lot of sense to me in terms of existence, cross-cultural beliefs about a life well lived, *crossing over* from this existence to the next, and most surprising to me of all—I think it makes much of the ancient literature found in places like the Bible even more brilliant.

32

Right and Wrong

The traditional religious definitions of right and wrong are easily condensed to a basic formula: What God likes and commands is good, and everything that opposes those things is bad. As long as thought is encapsulated in a single religion and limited to things the texts say that God has declared, this is a simple and straightforward system. However, if more than one religion is consulted the results are immediately problematic. Students of world history know the commands of different religious texts can and have led members of different faiths to kill each other with all involved believing they are doing what is right by the declarations of God. Even within religions, problems arise when decisions must be made about things not discussed in the accepted texts. Where God has not spoken, man is left to extrapolate and interpret God's meaning from other aspects of recorded revelation. Any basic study of religion will demonstrate that there is little agreement across varieties of the same religion. Further, ancient commands are easy to dismiss as outdated when they do not match current understanding. Few people today believe that eating a shrimp is worse than eating a cow. On the other hand, old beliefs are easily accepted when they match continuing prejudice. For example, LGBTQ behaviors remain abominations for many in hetero-male–dominated organizations. Attempts to find *universals* by reading across texts fail not only across different religions but within the interpretations of the same religions.

The biblical text of Genesis goes so far as to label action taken by the first people to gain this understanding of what is right and wrong as the cause of all suffering and the introduction of evil into human experience.

WHAT DOES CURRENT SCIENTIFIC KNOWLEDGE OF THE UNIVERSE SAY?

First, the very terms right and wrong are problematic because of their long-standing implication that some universal standards for behavior have been found or revealed. They have not. However, science shows that there are ways that matter and energy move and interact and ways that they do not. To be sure, situations still occur where observation does not agree with human predictions based on previous experience and theory. This leads not to explanations of some part of nature being evil, or contrary to the laws of most of nature, but to further research until understanding is gained of the forces involved in the new phenomenon.

Something like right and wrong may be found by observations that seem to support the traditional teachings of the Eastern world. Behaviors which match the known actions of matter and energy will bring harmony with what is, while behavior that defies known laws of science will logically lead to undesirable results. At the most basic levels this is as simple to understand as it is hard for human beings to practice. Acceptance of what is and living in simplicity lead to tranquility. Desiring more than we need or things other than the normal order of nature leads to agitation and possibly destruction. This should give us pause when efforts to force others into our models of right and wrong, or natural and unnatural, cause demonstrable patterns of pain and suffering.

Good and evil however are difficult labels to apply. Working to be completely at peace with anything and everything that is could mean taking no action to change the world, to fight injustice, or to improve the conditions under which we live. It is our agitation with the unknown and the unexplained observation that drives the scientific endeavor itself. Humans want to know and understand. Modernity was based upon progress through understanding possibilities and exploiting them, even while ancient texts label the desire for things to be other than what is as the source of suffering.

Much depends upon the scale and location of the observation. Gravity always works. Then humans develop the capacity to travel beyond the atmosphere and live in conditions where it does not work in the small scale created inside the capsule. Nevertheless, gravity continues to hold that capsule in dependable orbit around Earth even while appearing to act in new ways in small demonstrations. Two physical objects like pool balls can accurately be predicted to behave in certain ways when struck in the same way. However, when one begins to explore the molecular and atomic levels, actually striking the matter of the pool balls never occurs. At the subatomic level, matter becomes quanta of energy and the pool balls do not even exist in the manner which most people understand the meaning of the terms. Quanta of energy are occurring in complex relational realities forming an apparently stable formation described as a pool ball. But those subparts cannot be forced to behave in the same way as the total ball.

In configurations labeled as *living*, the complexity is multiplied exponentially. The subject of our observation may divert the blow, move in the direction indicated, or retaliate. In living organisms, the patterns of energy and energy transfer reach a level of complexity often rendering prediction impossible. This does not mean that things are behaving differently than in the non-living world. It means that the level of complexity of interactions exceeds current levels of comprehension and prediction. To circle back for a moment, this may be seen to parallel Eastern teachings about not trying to change things that cannot be controlled or changed. One finds greater synchronicity with other living things when the behavior of the other is known and accepted than when attempts to manipulate and change behavior are in play. And it makes little difference whether one's methods are scientific or magic. So, it is tempting to label behavior which coincides with the observable patterns of what is as *good*, while acts that break pattern might be seen as nonproductive, harmful or *bad*.

SOCIAL CONSTRUCTS

Far easier to understand on a macro level are the conventions formed by groups. Human beings use religion, reason, habits over time, and force to establish patterns of behavior deemed to be *right* or *wrong*. Animal groups establish hierarchies of power, life-protecting patterns, and regularities of behavior that closely parallel human rules of manners such as eating order. Explaining how the subatomic quanta combine into the molecules, cells, organisms and collectives that exhibit these behaviors is beyond the reach of current human explanation. For now, it is advisable to examine them on the observable level.

Unified Field Theology

Because human beings are able to communicate the internal processes we label as thought and beliefs with each other, group constructions are possible. These constructions may be the most practical understanding of right and wrong. To be sure, these conventions are given extra power when attributed to an all-powerful being. But, in everyday life their enforcement occurs on the human level. It is human behavior which enforces the agreed upon standards of behavior, even when the original source is claimed to be divine. And these constructions vary across groups and across time. One finds harmony by being aware of and aligning one's behavior with what is *right* or *wrong* within the social setting. The successful child from a high poverty neighborhood often learns very different rules and definitions for home, the street, and the school or church. The religious business person may function according to very different standards of behavior according to whether they are in the religious or the business environment. The same can be said to be true of the religious academic. This is problematic and labeled by terms such as hypocrisy when the starting place is an assumption of universal standards. When the constructions are allowed to stand on their own merit, there is no problem. Humans learn to coexist and succeed by matching their behaviors to the somewhat dynamic standards of behavior of the groups within which they function. What is right or wrong in this place is right or wrong in this place and at this time until new constructions are imposed or constructed.

Here the apparent internal logical inconsistency of the Bible itself may be examined. If the pronouncements of right and wrong evolve throughout time as the groups whose stories are told grow and evolve, a very interesting narrative of human intellectual history emerges. Early on what is *us* and for *us* is right and what is against *us* is wrong and to be opposed, even to the point of killing entire populations of other human beings. As agreements about what constitutes proper and improper behavior evolve and change, one finds the prophetic voice opposing and offering a counter-narrative to the ruling voice. Promises of blessings become extended to all who follow the rules for right living and instructions to share those blessings increase. At the time of the *pax romana*, where the authorship group finds itself as the *other* oppressed by conquering powers, thoughts on correct behavior evolve to include teaching that one is to be kind, even to love one's enemies. When the temple in Jerusalem is destroyed in AD 70, the literal sacrifices of Judaism which must be performed at the temple, are transformed to acts of personal sacrifice and the performance of *mitzvahs*.[1] As a narrative of human understandings and joint constructions about what is acceptable behavior, the ancient texts are fascinating and informative. If God is seen as fully known and understood at each point in the narrative, the evolution of thought contradicts the concept of an unchangeable God. However, a God who is the force of the universe will surely be understood in different ways at different times as both knowledge and circumstances change.

Early human beings, faced by many threats to life, developed early constructions that told them that they were good, and the continued life of their group was good. It even makes sense for these early constructions to label questioning these rules and wanting to form individual theories as the source of trouble and thus as evil. As man gains greater control over the environment, dependability of food supply, and protection from natural forces and other groups, the constructions can evolve without threatening the existence of the group. The force originally seen as commanding life and death loyalty to the survival of small social groups is later understood to be more benevolent not just to the specific group, but to the rest of life.

---

1. Adar, "Where Do You Sacrifice the Animals?"

33

How It All Fits

We now know that the universe creates itself from what we call nothing. This potential field is everywhere (omnipresent), is the source of all energy and everything that we call matter (omnipotent), and while assumptions of knowledge have a history of anthropomorphic error, since nothing exists apart from this source it can be said to *know* all things (omniscient).

We live in a time when science may in fact have shown the existence of that power, that potential for everything, that is the reality behind religious constructions called God. It is difficult to describe in simple English but elegantly expressed in the language of mathematics. Each new generation of experimentation and observations in both the subatomic and astronomical realms confirms that it is real. The universe *is*, and is self-explanatory.

From this new vantage point we may reconsider the wisdom of the past. The collapse of the Western narrative of a biblical God who set up a system of crime and punishment where God alone could serve the penalty and offer forgiveness only to those who know certain facts and accept certain teachings opens a door to new understanding. Since the Bible makes it clear that most of earth's human occupants lived and died with no knowledge of those specifics, the Bible does not support the supposition that universal meaning can justly be based only on acceptance of that dogma or theology. What is pervasive in the text is the wisdom to understand that we are not the authors of the universe and are indeed quite small. So, humans should live with humility and appreciation of the wonders that surround us. Further, understanding that man is not the creator calls for care, or at least a lack of abuse, toward the rest of humanity as well as the rest of the world. We are not the makers, so we do not have the right to destroy. We recognize our limits and the risk to our existence. We recognize that life is better when we care for those in need. The words of the ancient prophet that man should "act justly, love mercy, and walk humbly"[1] seem to be very wise advice after all.

Perhaps we may even reconsider the meaning of the Genesis narrative. Man emerges as part of the natural world at the end of a list of sequentially arriving physical and living forms that matches surprisingly well with what science observes in the geologic record. But, the human mind is capable of a kind of reasoning that permits a conscious decision to separate from the rest of nature and see ourselves like gods and able to judge the worthiness of other things. And there we are—separated from intimate relationship with the rest of what is, because we chose it. This is very different from saying humans were banished for disobeying a judgmental God. The explanation for our isolation from the rest of nature is that we chose to be separate and nothing has been the same since. The rest of the Judeo-Christian texts, along with teachings from the full diversity of global humanity, read in this context of trying to find our way back to unity with the universe that *is* will speak to us in ways very different from recent US evangelical interpretation.

- Tower of Babel—as humanity continues to try to rise above all other life on earth, humanity is separated from and turns on itself to a degree requiring each group to have a distinct language to recognize their own.[2]
- Abram—hears something that calls him to move apart and instead of an important person in his homeland becomes known as Abraham, the father of two major ethnic groups.[3]
- Moses—recognizes injustice in Egypt and when compelled to return and act demands a name for the power that sends him. The answer is the first person for what is, *I am*.[4]
- Israel—kings, usually with support of the priesthood, live lives of accumulation and oppression occasionally interrupted by the appearance

---

1. Micah 6:8.
2. Genesis 11.
3. Genesis 11–17.
4. Exodus 3:14.

of prophets declaring that life well lived is about humility and caring for those in need.[5]

- Jesus—continuously teaches that the kingdom of God is here and evident in everyday stories of life and moments of joy commonly referred to as parables.[6]
- Paul—teaches that there are no social differences between people of faith, but also provides explanations about the teachings and rules for participation that become a religion like other religions.[7]

EXODUS 3 "I AM"

In the tradition within which I was raised, the creative force interacts with humans, calls certain humans to follow it in certain ways, favors those who do, and destroys those who do not. But, it never really works. Sometimes the faithful suffer. Both Jews and Christians have the ancient poem of Job who suffers incredible pain and loss through no fault of his own in a world he must admit he cannot explain. The Hebrew descendants of Abraham, the one both Jews and Muslims identify as chosen by the Creator, fall into slavery to a foreign power because of actions taken to avoid starvation. Suffering for those chosen for favor in the Jewish tradition continues until a reluctant liberator arises. It is this character in the narrative that first asks the power behind all things for a name.

The answer, I now believe, contains a powerful way to view the universe revealed to us by science. This answer freed from human characteristics and favoritism for one group of humans over all others offers a simple path of great value. It resonates with science which now tells us that the universe is what it is because it is consistent with what it is. The universe is because in all the reality we can observe, energy and matter manifest themselves in consistent ways. We know them as being and recognize them as belonging to categories we have created because their interactions are consistent with what they are. The universe simply *is*.

If we take *what is* and place it in an anthropomorphized narrative like the ancients, we can ask it questions. Moses can ask *what is* its name. And the expression of *what is* now needs to be placed in the first person for a

---

5. 1 Kings—2 Chronicles.
6. Matthew—John.
7. The Epistles.

reply that makes sense in our languages. The first-person reply for *what is* becomes, *I am*. The Jewish and Christian narratives record this as the ancient answer. The teachings of Buddhism guide the student toward letting go of a self-centered, pain-avoiding worldview to accept oneness with what is. Many teachings of Native Americans avoid defining the Creator as any one thing and tell us that the Creator is in all things and all things are one in the Creator. So perhaps it has been there all along. The explanation for the universe revealed by science shows that it is because it is. It does what it does because natural processes are consistent. It does not conform to our magic, our rituals, or our wishful thinking because it simply does what energy and physical manifestations of energy do under similar conditions. When we force human language onto this force, which is far beyond anything human, it says to us in all our bewilderment and grasping, *I am*.

JOB 7:17 "WHAT IS MAN?"

In Jewish and Christian traditions, man is made of earth and the breath of God. Natives of the continent we call North America say that we are children of Mother Earth and Father Sky. Science says we are elements of the planet Earth combined in ways that express the energy known as life.

The first explanation has been used to assert that we are unique from and superior to all other combinations of earth and energy. Sometimes this has been expressed in ways we like to call good when humans act as caretakers for earth and all life found here. However, it has also been used to justify humans acting as owners, manipulators, users and destroyers of all else that is within our reach. The aboriginal beliefs of our continent have been kinder, including both the use of other life-forms for sustenance and respect for them as equal expressions of what is. The scientific position has traditionally claimed to be value neutral. While the Judeo-Christian view sees each individual's existence as beginning at birth—and in more recent times at conception—both scientific and aboriginal beliefs note that we are new combinations of elements that have been here since time began and which will continue after our current form is gone. Religion, which sees the human physical form as definitive and temporary, depends on explanations of heavens and eternal states to answer our need for significance.

Twenty-first-century scientific understanding of human life as an expression of the same elements and forces as all other things may offer a new understanding of existence already present in the poetic statements of the ancients. We are dust, for a time we are animate, and in the end, we are again dust as our energy rejoins the energy outside our being. It would be a grand mystery indeed if we were made of something other than the elements of the planet that houses us. Genetics traces common markers in all of us back to common ancestors even though the specific molecules containing that evidence have been replaced many times over. We are now at a time when science tells us that the energy and the matter expressed as our being have been here since the beginning and will continue while the universe continues to exist. To be sure, they have been and will be found in many combinations strange to us. But everything that is identifiable as us is as continuous as the universe. Is this the vision of Siddhartha inviting humans to come to terms with and find joy in the fact that we are but one manifestation of what is, and that we will remain part of what is reunited with the general field of being when our current state ends? There are worse ways to see life.

PSALM 133 "HOW GOOD AND PLEASANT IT IS TO DWELL TOGETHER"

One of the strongest forces maintaining my childhood paradigm was fear that all basis for common life and decency would disappear if the laws of God as interpreted from reading the Bible were no longer acknowledged as divine commands. I have heard many arguments that without the laws of God as given to the ancient Israelites and interpreted by US Christian churches there would be chaos with no moral distinction between charity and murder. From inside the worldview that the directions for living correctly are determined by God and given to men in literal forms, the argument makes sense. Considered from a larger view of existence and human history, other possibilities emerge.

Life forms gather together with similar life-forms and behave in ways that are beneficial to all with no instruction from ancient texts. Living things gather together in herds, flocks, schools and forests. Together they locate and share resources, protect each other from predators and weather the storms of the planet. There is no need to teach them laws given from outside of natural reality. Collectivity and cooperation work; therefore, they happen.

I also find it interesting that the same appears to be true in the elements of earth that are not commonly considered as living or mobile. When gold is found, there is a higher probability that more gold is nearby. Minerals are found in veins and large-scale deposits. Science will tell us that it is because the geological area has a common history and has been exposed to common forces. In the case of carbon-based formations, the area was once inhabited by common life-forms. There is no magic or grand design required, and perhaps I am making too much of it as well. But, it seems clear that in the natural world like things are found together, and those that can be observed act in ways that are mutually beneficial. I see no reason to assume that humans should require more magical outside protection from chaos and destruction than the rest of life.

But the aberrant does occur. From the molecular to the macro levels, life appears in ways that do not match the existing norms. When the unusual forms are harmful to the other individuals or the collective, we want answers and solutions. We want to know that the world makes sense. So, it is perhaps comforting to believe that there is a supreme presence that declares what is correct and what is not, that defines for us what is right and what is wrong. But, this is problematic at best in human behavior given the number of times it is precisely the adherence and loyalty to one religious expression over all others that has led to destructive behaviors.

And we know most of the time whether our behavior is consistent with expectations or contradicts them. My own theory of rules and laws is that they are to justify the way in which we wish to treat those who deviate. Even children know when their behavior is likely to please or irritate peers or authority figures. Rules seldom make the difference in how they behave. They act out of reasoned choice or momentary emotion, but seldom through mental checking of the rule book. The rules simply justify adult reactions to them. The same applies to those individuals who will choose behaviors destructive to others. Neither the rule of God or man prevents the aberrant from being aberrant. Such beliefs only comfort the rest of us as we justify our chosen response to the distasteful behavior.

Nevertheless, most of the time species including humans can be seen forming collective groups which behave in ways that are advantageous to the group. As sense-making organisms, we observe the behaviors and assemble theories about them by looking backward at what has occurred over time.

I recently did a thought experiment on the topic in real time as I observed the behavior of a variety of drivers who happened to be traveling the same direction at the same time on an interstate. None chose to be there with the others except that we all chose a time of day and the most convenient method of travel in a similar direction. And still, rules that resembled those of community could be constructed. There were amounts of space considered adequate to maintain between vehicles, common methods of signaling changes in behavior, and ways of moving in order to allow differences in speed of travel without collisions to name a few. Working backward, we can identify social laws, rules and mores that were in effect. We could force the behavior into patterns to match our ideas of community or competition. But, mostly, a group of humans traveled a common path in ways that benefitted each member of the species present at that time consistent with the normal behaviors observable in nature.

34

The Cross and Suffering

After another day of humans killing other humans in an act of terror, I watched people on my social media feeds discuss why they displayed unity with France but failed to do so with Kenya, Beirut, and other targets of hatred. At least one person responded that Facebook made it easy to do France by giving a colored icon option. I think there is truth in that as well as in the posts that point out how we respond more when people we see as *us* are suffering.

The logical next question is what to post to show your empathy for and unity with all who suffer due to the hatred of others, or maybe with all who suffer for any reason. And, I think again that Christianity could have been an answer. The faith I was raised in could have presented the world with a powerful symbol of compassion. But, we made it about vengeance and blood payment for wrongs.

The cross that Christianity has offered the world has been presented too many times as the place where a bloodthirsty God is satisfied by the death of God's Son in repayment for the disobedience of eating a piece of fruit. Emphasizing the story in this way easily leads man to see the cross as a symbol of punishment, even of bloodthirst and vengeance. If the God of all the universe is primarily seen at the cross as the one who demands death payment, what violence is man not justified in taking on other men in response to serious offenses whether real or perceived?

But, there could have been a different framing of the story. What if Christ is seen as God willing to do anything and take every step to be in unity and harmony with man? What if we consider the God who loves the creation so much that God is willing to suffer everything creation suffers, even death? Now the image is not about brutal justice. It is about joining humanity in our pain.

If the cross is a symbol of vengeful violence, then it becomes just one more image of the hate that is killing people every day.

If the cross is a symbol of the God of the universe suffering all that man suffers in order to be united with us, does it not represent the attitude we would desire in these times? Jesus on the cross calling out, "Why have you forsaken me?"[1] becomes a brother to every human being faced with the isolation of helplessness in a world of chaos. And that Christ should call all followers to do likewise. That Christ asks us what price we will pay to be in fellowship with *all* who suffer.

Theologians can discuss how the cross may be both and which is most accurate to the message of truth. I am contemplating the image presented to the world, not the complexities we play with in academic discussions and training.

I fear that a bloodthirsty God willing to accept the sacrifice of its own offspring presents to the world an excuse for every human violence committed as retribution for wrongs previously suffered. The cross presented as a symbol of such a deity will be nothing but offense to those who are in conflict with those who wear this symbol.

I can identify with a Creator who suffers all the pain that befalls its creation. I can relate to a God who would pay any price to rescue creation from evil and suffering, a God who is willing to be us, walk with us and suffer with us. If the message of Christianity had been framed as such unlimited love, maybe, just maybe, there would have been crosses instead of French flags trending on social media.

Maybe. The way things are now, the cross is a symbol of one set of armies in a world doomed to watch story after story of how we destroy each other. But maybe, those who wear it had another choice. And I wonder if that choice might still be reclaimed.

The icon I chose to post was John Lennon's plea to imagine a world where we put all the religions aside and recognize our brotherhood in a world we do not understand. Raised and ordained in Christianity, I wish I could have posted a cross in the knowledge that any who saw it would have

---

1. Matthew 27:46.

identified with a message of limitless love, unity and brotherhood in suffering. But current theology is the antithesis of a unified field.

35

Overwhelmed by Size

We pursue our quest for meaning in a universe science has now revealed to be so large that we seem inconsequential. Current estimates say the universe contains at least two trillion (2,000,000,000,000) galaxies, each containing numbers of stars beyond our normal ability to comprehend.[1] The central place of earth beneath a canopy of visible stars, which was already a number so large that "as numerous as the stars"[2] was used by the ancients to describe quantities too numerous to count is gone. We learned long ago that the sun and heavenly bodies do not revolve around us. Now we know that stars, planets, and other objects exist in such quantities and at such distances that it is hard to imagine our planet or anything on it as significant when measured against the whole. Unfortunately for us and our desire for meaning, that includes us.

Having become self-aware, we want to believe that our thoughts, beliefs, actions and lives matter. We would like to believe that they continue to exist past a number of decades we can usually count on our fingers. And then we look out at the vastness. With all of its grandeur and beauty, it still refuses to affirm that we matter on our watery little rock on one sidearm of the Milky Way. Who are we in comparison to the size and complexity within our own galaxy, let alone two trillion or more? Looking up can lead to quiet despair even during our appreciation of the beauty. We really are very small after all.

1. Galeon and Marquart, "Universe Is Far Bigger."
2. Genesis 22:17.

Overwhelmed by Size

We adopt forms of government and declare them superior to all others. We inherit and pass along religious teachings which allow us to claim to know the power behind it all and the one truth revealed for all mankind. We divide ourselves by race, location, nation and belief proclaiming various forms of superiority. We go to war over our lists and kill vast numbers of our own species. We take every resource of the planet and use it no matter how much damage we realize we are causing to the earth, ourselves, and all other planetary life-forms. And we want to believe that all our building, investigation, theorizing, sense making and violence in the name of truth are both justified and have ultimate meaning.

The heavens remain what they are and refuse to speak back the assurance we desire. Only the size and quantity answer and tell us that we are very small and the cosmos can continue with no pause without us.

36

Humility and Gratitude Affirm Existence

So much depends upon where we choose to begin. We may just as easily begin with the life-sustaining properties of the universe and our planet. To my mind, it changes everything.

When we look to the skies and desire to see a magic and all-powerful version of ourselves, we are disappointed. We see vast expanses filled with wonders beyond our comprehension which leave us feeling insignificant. But, that is impression not fact. What we see out there is exactly what we are made of down here. Everything we are in substance and energy is provided from out there. Everything we see out there is made of the same packets of energy become matter that comprise our own physical reality. Each and every day the sun continues to shine new energy which is absorbed by the systems of our planet which warm, feed, and sustain us. We can just as easily say that it requires hubris to label indifferent that which like a doting mother continues every day to pour out for us everything we need to grow and become who we are.

The sense of meaninglessness, our orphaned feelings of futile abandonment in the immensity of it all, come when we insist in finding out there a reflection of ourselves. If we allow the universe to be what we know it to be, it fulfills many of the characteristics we have called God from the time of the ancients. The universe provides the source of life, the sustaining power of life, and our destination at the end of life. We come from it, live within it, and in the end we return our energy and our substance to it. It is both the source and destination of all that we are and own. It inspires our

Humility and Gratitude Affirm Existence

contemplation of beauty and surprises us by being always more than what we have imagined. And all good gifts come to us from it. We experience life as good and discover the wonders it reveals. And we have cause to be grateful.

What it refuses to do is be human. Good theology has always tried to proclaim that God is not the same as us, is spirit, is beyond our limits of body and mind. And yet, our religious efforts have always insisted on turning the ultimate into something cartoonists easily draw as one of us grown old and wise. The heavens provide no such image. They give life, wonder, beauty, awe, and everything that is. They are the source and ultimate destiny of everything we know. But, they refuse to be a mere reflection of us.

Does our small existence imply meaningless existence separated from the grandeur of the universe? Only when we ignore the gentle rain, the warming sun, the welcoming sea, and the glorious light filling the vastness and demand instead to see ourselves.

37

"Faith Is the Substance of Things Hoped For"[1]

This week I was fortunate enough to have dinner with an old classmate and two of our mentors, Don Janzen and Don Pitzer. These two men from the study of anthropology and history specialized in efforts to build meaningful communities. They opened our eyes to new ways of viewing the past, the present, and human efforts to build better lives. Possibly in anticipation of our meeting, I was shocked one evening to think of the verse above in a way I had never read it before. I told them laughingly that Mother Ann Lee, founder of the Shakers, had sent me a revelation through the second coming of Marshall McLuhan, who coined the phrase "The medium is the message."[2]

For the first time, it hit me that this famous verse, memorized early and encountered often in sermons and theology, says that faith is the substance. I have always heard this Scripture as a statement that faith is evidence that there is something more than the material, that the spiritual is real, and that the eternity we hope for beyond our mortal forms is real. But, it does not say that faith proves something else. It says that faith is the thing hoped for modified also by the phrase "the evidence of things not seen."[3] We like that second part; it confirms what we want it to say and the first phrase is

1. Hebrews 11:1 KJV.
2. McLuhan and Fiore, *Medium Is the Message*. Note that in the book title the word message was, possibly by accident, changed to massage.
3. Hebrews 11:1 KJV.

often translated, faith is the *assurance* rather than the *substance*. The Greek word is *hypostasis*. When I look it up out of context, I find the "underlying reality or substance."[4] I know that words out of context can be dangerous in translating the meaning and intent of an entire passage. I also know that the word standing alone avoids the temptation of the scholar to define the word according to their paradigm for the passage under consideration. So, I also looked up the word for evidence in the second phrase and found *elegchos*,[5] which refers to proof through reasoning, and oddly seems to appear more often in Bible texts as disproving or convicting of error. What if we consider this verse accordingly; faith is the substance we hope for, the reasoned explanation of things unseen? Or, faith is the substance of our hopes and our chosen reasoning for what we do not see? It would seem then that faith is its own object. We cannot see the exact beginning of all things and faith tells us that what is came from something beyond what we can see. Science agrees based on reasoned analysis of what we can observe at the time of this writing. It simply does not agree to anthropomorphize that which is unseen. We cannot see the future and so we trust our faith, or confidence, in what we have decided through questioning and reasoning that what we cannot yet see is trustworthy. Science predicts future events based on observations in the past and present, and our assurance of its accuracy is based on our confidence in the logic and consistency of the reasoning presented.

Marshall McLuhan reminds me that the way we receive the message may be both the actual message and the massage that comforts us as we encounter the message.[6] I now see the strong possibility that this long-quoted verse follows a similar pattern. We sit beneath the cosmic vastness amid what seems to be eternity and we reason about what we hope to be true. Our faith in our conclusions is the result. Our confidence that we understand something of our place in the universe, that the meaning and relationships we construct have value, that we are where and what we should be in the order of things, is the end result. It is what we live by and where we take comfort.

The fundamentalist will immediately reject this as heresy contradicting the revelation of every word in the particular version and passage of the Bible they choose to use and trust. Still, we have no proof of any reality

---

4. Google dictionary online, s.v. "hypostasis."
5. *Strong's Bible Concordance* (at BibleHub.com), s.v. "elegchos."
6. McLuhan and Fiore, *Medium Is the Message*.

Unified Field Theology

beyond our own. We have no proof that we live beyond the moment when our energy returns to the cosmos. We accept or deny those things based on our faith in the system of explanation that we find most convincing. The Christians of twentieth-century America took comfort in their confidence that there is a force outside the universe which gave them meaning and which would gather them home at life's end. Many continue to do so. But, for us who can no longer accept an interpretation of truth which denies each discovery of science; those of us who cannot read every word of ancient poetry, metaphor and myth as fact or prophecy; those of us who need to find a path to life within what we know, perhaps this verse has been calling all along.

I hope for a life well lived. My reason tells me that a life consistent with reality is superior to one based on things I cannot know. I have faith that my efforts to live as a human content with being is enough. As a human, I care about other human beings. As a thinking being, I care about the planet on which I live and the other life-forms on it. I am excited by new knowledge and the sheer experience of living. I am content. My confidence, or faith, in where reason has brought me becomes the confidence I hope for that my life makes sense as well. Understanding and meaning are our goals. The conclusions we draw and the confidence we have in them are the substance on which we build our lives. And as a result, faith in our thoughts and belief systems is its own substance.

38

Difficulty with the Label "Christian"

Few of my friends would suspect me of struggling with living under the label of Christian. But, I now confess.

Part of it comes every time I see a self-declared Christian proclaiming hatred for anyone who is not like them, or not like who they pretend to be—the LGBTQ community, the Muslim, the foreigner, the *other*. I hear it and want to proclaim loudly to the world that you must consider me to be outside that system if you wish to understand my heart and mind. Part of it comes when atheist friends online are friendly and open to my questions and treat me with respect as they answer my questions about how they see the world.

A bigger part comes while I see full evidence over and over, year after year, of the full existence of both heaven and hell right here in the actual universe we inhabit with the full knowledge that it is very often man who is choosing and causing which one is in evidence. How can I wait for a heaven somewhere someday while the society I live in and benefit from willingly places others in hell on earth both at home and abroad?

Part of it comes from studying too much and knowing that the view of God I was taught growing up was a very recent interpretation of ancient texts by and for the benefit of a very small group of my countrymen willing to condemn the rest of the world to eternal hell as long as they were reassured that they were now the chosen ones. As I now read more serious scholars, more ancient texts, and studies by authors within the Jewish

Unified Field Theology

tradition, I find the God I used to think I knew was worse than a myth. He was an evil myth in the self-interest of a narrow imperialistic group of people.

Part of my difficulty comes from the beauty of the universe itself and more convincing scientific arguments that it *is* possible for it to have come "from nothing."[1] The universe I live in contains all the beauty I need in the flickering light of the forest, the touch of ancient rock, the song of small birds, the cry of the hawk, and the endlessness of the night sky. I have known enough love, friendship, and joy of heaven here to be content if all that follows death is the return of my molecules to the natural cycles. I am at peace.

So, how can I be a Christian? The God who walks in human flesh and cries with human tears is the God I know. The God who proclaims that heaven is exemplified by a father who runs to welcome a foolish and rebellious son matches the God who walks with me. The God who proclaims that we have within us the power to fight back against the dark, the evil, the deadly, the nihil is my God. The strange power that comes to fill my heart with hope that things can be better, that humans can be more human, that light does shine in darkness when all my eyes can perceive is darkness, does not fit my categories of psychology, self-delusion, or whistling in the dark. When I am ready to give up, to fight back, to use the very weapons I oppose to try to stop at least some of the pain; it comes. The Christian language of the indwelling Spirit expresses well what happens when I need it most. The human who lived the life I most want to live, including being willing to die if it will rescue others, is Jesus of Nazareth.

I am sick of what the label Christian is used to mean in my day and time, and I have studied the past enough to know that other years and times were worse. I am content that I have been given so much grace that I do not need future magic to proclaim that my life has been good no matter how it ends from here. But, the inescapable truth that holds me when I can no longer hold on, that gives me strength to weep and work has no sweeter name in the lexicon of man than Jesus of Nazareth.

And still, the image of Jesus that only saves those who know about and accept him along with the dogmas that men attach to his teachings excludes too much of the world for me to accept it or to worship it. So, I live in the paradoxical space between what could be and current expressions of Christianity.

1. Krauss, *Universe from Nothing*.

39

Living the Paradox by Climbing Rocks

People ask why I climb rocks. Some even tell me to stop before I get hurt. So, why do I do it?

First, it is fun. My father taught me a lot about duty, honor, and responsibility. But, his most important lessons were about enjoying life and the importance of doing things that are fun.

Second, it is good for my body. I lost over thirty pounds without doing any kind of additional diet when I returned to regular climbing. And, I have added muscle tone I never had when I was young. My body responds to the exercise in very positive ways. For somebody who has been too uncoordinated for most sports all my life, that is a big deal.

Third, it connects me to some of the best times in my past. Memories flood back from camping, hiking, and climbing with my family and friends in that same forest and many other places during more than one period of wonderful years.

But, there is more. I am becoming more and more aware of the importance of an integrated life—living with mind, body, and soul in agreement. I have tasted spiritual life and know the difference of living with body and spirit unified. Climbing has made me more and more aware of how much time I spend divided.

I spent my career in Evansville with kids I can honestly say I loved and at the same time wished I was in Africa or Haiti. I sit at home with my family and my mind is at work, talking to distant friends on the internet, wandering distant mountains, or attempting to join Einstein's ride aboard

Unified Field Theology

the light beam as I visualize theories of subatomic and astronomical matter and energy.

I am in the presence of friends in conversation or study that feeds my soul, and my body is stretching finger tendons itching to be on the move—or deep in sleep. I love realizing the positive in me by seeing it reflected in health and well-being for others, but I also try to hide or deny the negative parts that are also very much me.

The examples go on and on.

But, on the rock I am me. I am present. My body, mind, soul, spirit—choose any fragment you want—are all there united in that moment of body, rock, water and air. My inner self soars with joy but only climbs as well as my body remembers to breathe and relax. My fears are there too. Not so much of injury, but of failure. Fear of not staying on the rock, losing ground I've already covered, letting down the friends I am climbing with, looking like the clumsy kid I always was. And it is OK. The fear is united with the need to breathe and the desire to climb toward the world of the hawk. It is all one.

It is all me; together, unified, present to the fact that all of life is present in that very moment, the next move of hand or foot, the next breath in or out, the next glimpse of beauty surrounding the rock, the flashing memories of love lived out, the sadness and loss of those who have been there with me before, the mourning of the summits real and metaphorical that I will not climb in this lifetime is combined with my thirst for more on every level of being, and it is all good because I am fully integrated.

For glorious moments of eternity I am unified with myself and the world and it is holy. Rock, water, air, body, and spirit are one and I am gifted to know and experience it. I return to other activities a more united being, less fragmented, more aware that this moment is. I am. We are. Even with every negative I am, I see, or I can imagine—life is, and it is as it should be. Each breath, thought and movement is synchronized in a moment of eternity. That holy moment is all I have or need.

Part of me reacts that it is too selfish to think of such an individual activity as a paradise. That is the division trying to remain. I answer it with truth that in many ways is beyond words. Every step on that rock is also a prayer for every child with mountains to climb, every peaceful breath affirms the rightness of peace for humanity, every thirst affirms our desire for more of life, more time together, more unity with all that is. We are after all, all on this rock together.

40

Death

My friend was killed along with other members of his family. It was sudden, inexplicable and unchangeable. The family shared a day of joy, followed by car problems that left them beside the road, and then the senseless impact that killed them. Pain rippled through our own community and many others.

As I have been working on these essays, I have also been telling people a bit too glibly that I am fine with simply returning my particles to the universe whenever the time comes. It is fine and comforting to hope for reunions somewhere beyond death, but we have no proof. I have been saying I am fine either way.

Then death happens to someone else. Somebody loved and mourned by many is suddenly gone. A wonderful family is gone in an instant and the question must be examined more closely. My childhood faith included a God who cared and watched out for even sparrows. His angels guarded and protected his precious children. I know I tested that theory too many times in very real experiments with rock climbing, exploring, and speed where a mishap would easily produce dire consequences. But, I was young and invincible and safely in the hands of a loving God. Then, a classmate died too young. A relative passed too soon. The years go by and more and more examples fill the memory of times when the magic didn't work, the angels did not intervene, and the innocent died. It happened again this week and it feels as if every cell in my body joins the mind in crying out, "Why?"

Unified Field Theology

The answer that has come to me may appear cold and uncaring, and perhaps strangely off track, at least in the beginning. When things collide with enough force, they come apart. This knowledge allowed man to construct the super colliders that have revealed so much about the foundation of everything we say exists. Even pieces so small they were once considered to be the indivisible prime objects explode when we strike them with other tiny particles at great speed. When a race car stops at the side of a track, even out of the place where cars normally drive and just close to it, the race is slowed or stopped because everyone understands that a stationary race car struck by another traveling at speeds nearing two hundred miles per hour will disintegrate. That is what happened to my friends. They were parked off but close to the traffic lane. Enter the next vehicle like a CERN particle and the resulting collision had very predictable results. That is how the universe works. The laws of physics do not depend on the goodness of those in the collision or how many people love them.

But where is this good God, angels, luck, or karma? We want to believe in a universe where those who do good receive good. We want to believe in a God who hears our prayers to protect our loved ones in their travels. We love the stories of the bad that almost happened but for the grace of God. The fact is that when we observe the world without blinders, it works the way it works and the very reason those special stories appear to be miracles is that they are not what usually happens.

If God is good when the second vehicle veers and misses, when the disease does not kill, when all are safe, then where or what is God when far more often the opposite happens? The famous Christian apologist C. S. Lewis spoke very honestly in his little book *A Grief Observed*, following the cancer death of his dear wife. When we are forced into the reality of loss, more than one of us has shared his greatest fear: not that God isn't real, but that God is real and fits none of our definitions of good.[1] Life ends. Every person said to be cured miraculously still dies of something. Storms, earthquakes, and tidal waves come in second to man's own acts of war and destruction. The bombs fall. The knock at the door comes. And no matter how many prayers are said, the bomb explodes where it hits. The terrorist kills *because* he heard prayers to a God who is not his God. Most of the time the magic does not work and where are we left in our desperation and grief?

---

1. Lewis, *Grief Observed*, 5.

Some can cling to the belief in an all-powerful God who could have protected and did not. Setting their own observations and pain aside they are able to rely on a belief that God knows. C. S. Lewis succeeded in doing this and returned to other writings on faith. Add the hope of a reunion beyond death and many cling to the comforts and assurances of their beliefs. But that faith, based as it is on ancient writing believed to be holy, is just that—faith, belief in something that cannot be known or proved.

And I sit here with my autonomous universe with no proof of this intervening God. Where am I left? With no proof that there is a God who saves some and fails the many, I am also free of the God who betrays us, tortures us, fails all the promises we were told were divine leaving us bereft. As surely as there is no proof of the universal rescuer, there is also no reason to believe in a cosmic sadist.

The universe does what it does. Our life choices expose us to dangers of speeding vehicles, radiation, toxic substances, and biologic agents and our bodies respond as bodies respond. Sometimes our body chemistry or strength overcomes the damage. Sometimes it cannot. Life is fragile. But, none of it requires a cosmic puppeteer, so we could conclude that it leaves us alone and without hope.

I would argue that it leaves us here on our beautiful blue marble together. Does life mean anything? Our own grief tells us how much our lives matter to each other. The very pain that seems able to crush us tells us how much we matter to each other. While daily business allows us to run past and take each other for granted, it is the very pain of loss that reminds us how vital many other people are to us and often motivates us to draw closer and communicate our caring. I do not need greater proof that humans matter. I know they matter each time a loved one passes or I witness the grief of others involved in the rituals of burying the dead. We matter to each other.

I find it hard now to believe that we matter to two thousand billion other galaxies or to any life that may exist in them. If we poison and overheat our planet and cease to exist, the rest of the universe will go right on working the way the universe works. But, that does not leave me hopeless. We matter to each other. I sit writing these essays because people I have never met but who may have struggled through similar life, knowledge and belief changes matter to me. We have never met, but we have much in common and I would bring them whatever since of meaning, belonging, and sanity my little essays on unified field theology might offer.

Do we matter in a universe this big? Watch the joy of a family with a new baby. Contemplate the happiness in the pictures they share. Solemnly observe those who suffer loss instead. See the importance of the other in their eyes; hear it in their words and cries; feel it in their tight embrace of a comforting friend. Know that we are not alone and meaningless; we are here observing a world beyond our own imagination or creation—together.

41

Death in Space-Time

This essay was prompted by another dream. If any of my old literalist, evangelical, or fundamentalist friends are still reading, they may take comfort in that. If they cannot accept the ideas here, they can assume that I have been listening to spirits other than the Spirit. I believe I have seen a reality which our common metaphors seek to soften and hide, but which has great value because it expresses truth about both existence and nonexistence.

The dream was simple. I was young and we were coming to the end of a visit with my maternal grandfather and some cousins. Dad was telling me it was time to give Grandpa a goodbye hug and then we had to go. And, I was crying because it was hard. Then, I woke up and realized that I was far more upset than a dream about life among family members I love should merit. As I took off my headphone speakers to get up and clear my head, Leonard Cohen's "So Long Marianne" was playing. Then I realized the dream was about death and permanent goodbyes, and a new understanding of that reality formed in my mind.

Raised within evangelical Christianity, all of our images and stories of death involved the loved one moving on to a new place where we would join them someday in the future. In hymns, sermons, and funerals it is a comforting idea. Bob Dylan expressed it on one of his overtly Christian albums in the song "Death Is Not the End." Johnny Cash wrote and recorded lyrics I love containing many of the images of my youth in the song "Far Side Banks of Jordan." The hymnals and songbooks of various denominations are filled with other examples. They offer more than a comforting image when memories of those already gone become painful. It is a promise I would like to leave with my own loved ones when I finish my own life. Unfortunately, it does not match anything we know or can confirm through science. It is a hope we can choose to cling to through faith. But, science gives a very different way of viewing the end of human life.

If the universe exists within a space-time continuum, then as we live we continue to move through that framework. When we cease to exist as living beings, we stop moving in space-time. Our loved ones carry our physical remains forward for a few days of comforting each other with reassurances of the teachings of faith, and then we commit the body to the grave and commend the soul to heaven. But the observable fact is that there the loved one remains in both time and space. The quanta that compose us begin the return to the universe and continue, but the person who was is now locked at a particular point in space-time. We have no confirmation that they journey into the future. That is the task that remains for us who live. Many times, I have heard in song and sermon about journeying through the "valley of the shadow of death"[1] as a task that must be completed on our own. From the viewpoint of science, we each die when our time comes but to my mind, the journey through the shadow remains for those who live. And it is a difficult one. We do not want to continue on without those who can no longer accompany us. For all of the fictions about time travelers preventing some great disaster or changing history, I suspect for many the fascination is in the possibility that we might go back to where that loved one is for the conversation we never had, or one more day of companionship and safety. But our task remains to journey forward along the arrow of space-time.

As I returned to bed and put back on my headphones, Bob Dylan was singing, "It's All Over Now, Baby Blue." The coincidence was not lost on my contemplation. I continued to think back to why the dream contained the images it did. Why were my still-living cousins also in the dream? And it came to me that it is not only the dead who we leave behind. Very often it is also the living we cease to see. A key family member, often the patriarch or matriarch, passes and the family ceases to gather. Each life becomes busy and there is no one there to call us all together to reaffirm the bonds of family and fellowship. We lose touch with the one who cannot journey further and with those whose paths simply diverge from our own.

Many years ago, I went on a backpacking trip along the continental divide. There was one valley in particular that became permanently

---

1. Psalm 23:4 KJV.

preserved in my memory after we camped there between a herd of elk and the pack of coyotes that was following them. With the smallest of efforts, I can call up the images and smells of that high-altitude environment. I have often used it in times of pain or high stress as a way to relax my body by taking my mind to a place of peace and beauty. I mention it in this context because there is always one addition to my memory. Sitting on a boulder on the far side of the valley, appearing happy and peaceful, but too far away to communicate, is always my paternal grandmother. I believe my mind and heart have chosen that favorite place as the location to envision her frozen in space-time. I can no longer go to her. I can go inside myself and picture her there in an environment that consoles me.

The only comfort in this middle-of-the-night awakening is that it matches my experience and observation. Instead of comforting images we can only hope are true, it affirms the reality of existence and fits within the universe we know. Having lived through six decades, I have watched many people who were vital to my journey reach their ending point and be left in memories of the past no matter how badly I desire them to be present now and in the future. This understanding of death as a stopping point in space-time confirms my experience including my own darkest moments.

I have often heard deep depression and suicide described as points where an individual can no longer see the possibility of a future. In my own moments of crises, the problem was not that the world would not continue, the pain was that it would. At my lowest points, the problem was a fear that I had absorbed all of life's pain I could withstand. The deepest angst was that tomorrow would bring another of life's burdens, tragedies, or betrayals and reach a level of pain beyond what my physical self could endure and remain. To stop at that time and place would not be because the future did not exist, but the very opposite. The future will arrive and there is a limit to how much loss one living being can endure and continue. Thankfully, each time I hit bottom, there was a person or an event which turned me back toward the joys and beauty that also arrive with each new moment. Life continues.

The songs which coincided with this nighttime reflection came from Apple's inexplicable algorithm composing a genius playlist to match a chosen song, Leonard Cohen's "Hallelujah." I love this song and its affirmation that even if everything falls apart, one can choose to stand in praise. That is the affirmation of life focused on the positive. Life does not have to work the way we choose. Life does not have to end the way we hope. Life does not have to continue endlessly for each individual consciousness. In fact, there are times when we realize endless existence would require exposure to more than humans can endure. There is comfort in the hope of a life beyond this one. There is also hope in realizing that after a life lived well there is a point in space-time that becomes our place to remain. In spite of all the lessons I heard, and taught, translating the Torah to be the Old Testament fully understood only through the lens of the Christian New Testament, I also find this perspective on life and death in the long traditions of Judaism from the ancients to today. The good life is one lived in right relationship to both the universal and those around us. The reward is a quality life and possible longevity. Then there is an end.

There we stay while others take up the tasks of life as humans being. There we remain in hope that those who continue take strength from the fact that we faced everything life brought with praise and gratitude.

42

How Much We Matter

I am still contemplating the possibility that given our miniscule size and location in the universe humans matter when we matter to each other, and cease to matter when we cease to matter to each other. When my daughters were born, I knew they mattered because they matter deeply to us, those who care about us, and all who came to care about them over the years. When anyone I care about dies, I confirm that they mattered in the painful clarity of how much they mattered to me. And yet, there is little evidence that it would cause the slightest ripple in the universe as a whole if we all stopped caring about each other and humanity destroyed itself. We matter when we matter to each other, and when we do not matter to each other, we do not matter.

It now occurs to me that with our current research and computation methods it might even be possible to quantify how much we matter. If we take the total number of people on earth times the total caring about others possible we would get a maximum range for how much humans matter. It would be the population squared assuming that all humans cared about all other humans.

The actual figure would predictably and regrettably be much smaller. If I do not care about the people of country X, the total would be reduced by my one times the population of that country. If I taught all of my daughters not to care about that country or one of its subclasses, the reduction in caring would be that population times five.

Unified Field Theology

Definitions of caring would be required. I grew up hearing people joyfully sing about how their Jesus loved the little children of every color. But, some of those same people had no problem with the destruction of entire villages in Vietnam if it furthered the aim of the United States being able to withdraw from that conflict as victors. So, definitions would be more complicated than simple statements of sentimentality. Do I care that you are alive? That you have the minimum necessities for life? Does caring require a concern that you are able to live with dignity, purpose, and freedom as your culture defines it? Definitions would be complicated.

But, within a given set of definitions, samples of the world population could theoretically be examined for caring about others of similar and different ethnicities, political persuasions, gender, religion, etc., and a theoretical number could be established for a time-specific estimate of how much human beings matter.

One part of me rebels already and asks, "Do we matter more or less if we also care about the rest of life on the planet and the potential of the planet to continue to sustain life?" For my worldview, I am very tempted to say yes, but that would lead us down the rabbit hole of how it matters beyond the caring of human beings about the issues and the longevity of our species. Refusing to add a magic external observer, issues which we consider vital are just part of the formula for how much we care about others who agree and disagree. So, this becomes only a category to be included in who I care about and how much. I care more about people who care about life and are willing to sustain it. So, the formula might become population times people cared about, times a numeric figure for how much we care about various populations.

The number is obviously too difficult to determine in a way that all audiences would agree is legitimate. Some religious folks would counter that humanity matters in an immeasurable quantity determined by how much we matter to a deity that cannot be measured. Thus, they would probably consider my number meaningless. Others would have their own preferences for categories to be considered rendering a consensus number largely impossible to reach. And it seems for a moment like I have taken this whole idea into a death spiral of non-meaning.

But, I do not agree that the mental exercise will fail us completely. I believe the very idea of a quantifiable amount of how much humanity matters determined by our beliefs and actions toward others has merit for human reflection. As I contemplate the existence of this difficult to calculate and defend number, I am drawn forward into its application.

If I watch the news of another natural disaster without enough concern to pause in consumption of my meal in front of the TV, I see the significance of the total human race reduced by the quantity of my indifference. The same happens as I recoil from stories of politics which cause me to devalue the people who support an ideology that is repugnant to me. Or, I can stop, reflect, and will myself to pay attention and see these others as more like me than they are different. To the extent that I renew my caring for them as human beings without requiring their acceptance of my own biases, I increase the value of the human race. Our imaginary number is increased (or decreased) by the amount of our increased (or decreased) concern times the number of those we are considering.

Perhaps there are those to whom such a concept would not matter. But, for those who came to understand it, what would be the effect on decisions about funding emergency relief for those in peril versus bombs to destroy everyone within blast radius of those labeled as our enemies? What if we realized that our very thoughts increase or decrease the total worth of humanity? What if we realized that decisions for violence and war, not only eliminate people we have declared unworthy but decrease the total value of humanity by our hatred or indifference times all those affected?

What if we finally agreed that instead of our place in the universe being determined by some magical spirit-being out there somewhere, the degree to which humanity matters fluctuates each moment according to us—our concern or hatred, our caring or indifference, our aid or violence?

Would we change in ways that would make us more human?

43

Expanding the Parameters of How Humans Matter

Contemplating the degree to which human beings care about each other has led me to further consider caring about, and caring by, other living things. Science now confirms what the ancients taught long ago. Other species are more like us than earlier science perceived. Animals care for each other, come to the aid of individuals in distress, and grieve the death of others. Animals kill for food to be sure. But, they do not kill in order to hoard for the future or to deny all consumption by other animals. Pet owners have long affirmed that animals show distress at the absence of owners, behaviors of guilt when caught misbehaving, and grief at loss. They grieve when we pass as we grieve their passing. Some studies have even dared to suggest caring and healing behaviors in plants. So, my hypothetical total of how much life on earth matters is increased as we gain understanding of how much life matters to nonhuman life-forms.

One has only to look at the use of pets as companion, service, and therapy animals in the United States, including programs bringing animals to comfort those in distress, to see that human feelings of self-worth increase in the company of comforting animals. The anecdotal evidence strongly suggests that human physical and mental health is improved through therapeutic relationships with domestic animals. The scientific data is less conclusive largely due to poor experimental design under the requirements of traditional research connected to claims of validity and generalizability.[1] Nonetheless, studies and anecdotal records showing improved health and emotional well-being abound. For my purposes here, the inference is strong that humans also matter because we matter to the animals which live among us.

On a purely physical level it is obvious that we matter because we have bred domestic animals to depend upon us for food, shelter, and health. This can easily be expanded to include house plants, while the link to general plant life remains a matter for further research. Having brought other life-forms into dependence on us, we matter to them for physical survival regardless of scientific controversy about psychological connections. To leave animals collected as pets uncared for is to commit the crimes of animal cruelty and neglect. We matter to these animals because we have caused them to become physically dependent on us through breeding and confinement.

Regardless of where one stands on specific claims of animal psychology, the anecdotal record adds another dimension to the significance of human existence based only on observable evidence outside of religious claims. We also matter because we matter to the rest of life on the planet. Humans establish deep and lasting relationships with other species. Other species come to our aid and protection. To the extent that we care for the earth, or at least limit our damage of it, other species thrive. When we abuse the environment for our temporary gain, or out of human hubris in environmental improvement through activities such as horticulture, forestry, and the damming of rivers, other species suffer, decline in numbers, or even become extinct. We matter to all of life on earth because our activities affect all life so profoundly that the current geologic period has come to be known as the Anthropocene Era.

My thoughts are mostly about the possible impact of becoming more aware of these relationships as the basis for our claims of significance. Humans claiming significance based on relationship to a God who exists outside of nature have committed acts of environmental destruction based on ideation of human superiority and rulership over the planet. To be fair, this is often in direct opposition to the teachings of the religions used. But, the idea of human separation from and authority over other life has led to negative human impact just the same.

I wonder how we might change if we came to value our own worth not only in terms of how much we matter to our own species, but in terms of how much we matter to all of life on our planet. Would we be less likely

---

1. Herzog, "Does Animal-Assisted Therapy Really Work?"

to continue destructive habits in agriculture and the extraction of minerals and petrochemicals if we understood that our value as a species declined each time we destroyed a habitat? Would we be less likely to collect domesticated animals in feed lots and factory style production barns if we understood that their suffering diminished our total worth? Would we be as eager to contemplate simply evacuating Earth to build a new human habitat on another planet if we understood our value as part of the total web of life on this planet?

Viewing myself as significant because I matter to the species and plants in my house, as well as to the other people, causes me to value my pets in a new way. They are part of my own existence. They wait for my return and rejoice in my presence and I see them in a new light as affirmation of my own significance. It is selfish and self-centered, but I believe healthier than seeing their worth only in terms separate from my own. Perhaps the families who mistreated and abandoned our current two dogs would still have them if they understood that their own value as human beings was increased by the affection of these animals for them. I do not know.

It does seem like a healthy view of life to see humanity as mattering not just to ourselves, but as part of the total biosphere. We matter because we are part of the entirety of the local and planetary ecosystems. We matter to those animals which become our close companions in ways which are at a minimum very similar to how we matter to each other. When we neglect, abuse, or destroy other life-forms, our own value as an earth species diminishes. When we increase the health of our relationships with the other forms of life which surround us, we become more valuable to them.

I suspect that we lost much of this awareness as our technologies of housing and travel increased. The very comfort in which we live and move also isolates us from life outside of our dwellings. Gathering millions of people together in cities isolated people from other life-forms except where they are artificially added to our brick and mortar environments. Vacations taken away from our large human hives are still spent in shelters which isolate most from direct contact with the very environments they go to visit. A few of us seek opportunities to go to the wild and experience it without surrounding ourselves with other people and constructed comforts. Some have begun to experiment with eco-villages and permaculture as real and sustainable life styles.[2] Many of us choose dogs or cats because we intuitively know that our life environment is richer because of their presence.

2. Lockyer and Veteto, *Environmental Anthropology*.

Expanding the Parameters of How Humans Matter

I believe it is time to reaffirm that the very value of our existence is tied to our relationships with each and every other life-form which shares our planetary home.

We matter because we matter to each other. And, our each other includes each and every one of our nonhuman neighbors. Perhaps expanding our definitions will make us better people. It might even make us better animals!

44

The End of Consumption

As a child of the sixties, I have long been aware of calls to limit human consumption and destruction of the planet. I have always agreed with these ideas although I have not always practiced my beliefs. I have fully participated in the consumer society where I was born. Although the form of Christianity I was raised within emphasized human responsibility to care for the earth rather than destroy it, we still behaved in ways more consistent with US society than ancient calls to shepherd all life on the planet. Now reconsidering the interplay of what we know and what we believe through these essays has caused me to contemplate another view of the issue.

From the moment of conception, humans are creatures of consumption. Starting with cells supplied by parents our bodies are built of materials filtered through or taken from our mothers. As toddlers, we shift to consuming food directly from the environment or created in chemical plants to mimic natural food. Then no matter whether we are total vegans, vegetarians, or eat a meat-based diet, every cell of our bodies is constructed of consumed materials. What we call food production is based on using assets of the earth to increase the growth of products we desire for consumption. The entire process is consumptive of planetary resources no matter what sleight of hand we include in our language about it. We produce nothing; nothing that isn't made from parts we consume from the planet.

We live in buildings made of materials from the planet, travel with fuels extracted from the ground, and entertain ourselves with energy taken by various modes from earth environments. Even our use of power sources such as water, wind, and sunlight use greater amounts of resources than we initially hope as we continue to study the actual production of our collection methods and the effects of our energy collection on the natural systems we utilize. Even while we speak of being great producers of everything that humans need and want, we actually take it all from the natural systems we inhabit. We are always, always consuming.

Until, I suddenly see death in a new way. When the breathing and the heartbeats stop, we notice the end of movement of any kind and the body temperature drops. The traditional view is one of watching what was, often what we treasured and loved as a family member or fellow citizen, slip away. One of my editors for these essays asked me if I knew of any quantitative data on what ceases to be at death. I did not, and it took a while, but it led to these thoughts. What ends at death is our consumption of the environment we inhabit.

As the body temperature drops energy is already returning to the surrounding space. We are finally giving back. If organs are shared, we recognize that the person who has passed has given something vital to another, still-living and consuming, person. The more naturally we allow the body to decay, the more completely we then give back all of the physical components that have been us, to the world that sustained and delighted us. Of course, the United States and many other societies do not like this ending. Family members may feel compelled to continue to consume on our behalf using up land space or constructing tombs to hold our physical remains in the most intact form for the longest possible time. But, the giving back continues nonetheless.

The quanta of energy that occupied space in a form that others could turn to and recognize as us, continue to rejoin the rest of the quanta of the cosmos. Energy that was always just passing through our space continues to do so uninterrupted by our finally quieted desires. We are at last, when all intentional action is gone, contributors rather than consumers.

Perhaps there is depth to be explored in this concept that only in death do we finally become contributors to, rather than consumers of, the world that surrounds us. I find it both humbling and comforting. Death is but the moment when we stop taking and begin returning all we have borrowed to the source.

45

The Wormhole

As I contemplated the role of humans as consumers in life, it occurred to me that I might be giving greater agency to choose consumption than I was explicitly saying. It is in our nature to consume, and as long as we live we continue to absorb matter and energy from our environment. Thinking about this further suggests another possible lens. It occurs to me that life may be thought of as a kind of gravity.

Biologists have long sought the mechanisms or explanations for how molecules can attract other molecules in ways that become self-replicating and thus begin the existence of what we know as life. Perhaps, from the very beginning, these complex molecules exhibit something like gravity on the world around them drawing others to themselves. Perhaps that is what life does, attract more matter and energy to itself as surely as do objects we do not consider living. Everything is made of the same basic quanta at the bottom level, and there may be no reason for nature to act differently in things considered living or nonliving by man.

In this view, it is a basic function of life to constantly attract the required elements to itself. Then at some level of complexity, what we know as awareness develops and the gathering seems intentional. But, what if it is in our nature as surely as it is for heavenly bodies and black holes? Continually pulling resources toward our beings, might be as natural as the attraction of adjacent items into the black hole. It might be the nature and *gravity* of life to pull in the continuing new supply of needed life energy. This view suggests two things that currently interest me.

First, consumption would not necessarily require the labels and stigma of greed which it has been given by both religion and environmental science. Granting that humans seem to have evolved a capacity beyond other earth forms to over gather, the basic process itself may be at the core of what it means for something to be alive. I do not believe it means we have to accept the destructive over-consumption we now observe; because, we have the same capacity for awareness of excess that we do for basic needs. But it might point us again to realizing that all humans must have access to the basic matter and energy requirements of life within their environments or perish. I would argue that it applies to all life-forms. Life draws the energy for life to itself, and every other form has the same need to do so as we humans.

We live our lives much like black holes, constantly drawing our environment into ourselves. The attraction and collection is inevitable and part of the definition of being alive. Considering that life often draws into itself matter, energy, or other life-forms that are detrimental rather than helpful, the environmental attraction might be seen as blind as the gravity surrounding the black holes we now know are ubiquitous in the universe. This view of our consumptive nature suggests to me that we are more different from the astrological objects quantitatively than qualitatively. We draw everything in toward us because it is how things work.

So, what is death? Perhaps death is the wormhole that many suspect inhabits the black hole. At death, all that life draws to itself reemerges on the other side—not a spiritual other side in the traditional sense, but a very real escape from the gravity of one life to the endless possibilities of new forms and other life. This parallel view to the end of consumption also seems hopeful and reassuring to me as we begin to understand that we are a strange and consuming collection of energy for a very short cosmological time. When our time is done, that collection emerges for recombination and rejuvenation as life leads to life even as individual forms come and go. I believe that our current knowledge of the universe viewed through unified field theology allows us to see that it is in the hour of our death that we return to complete unity with our source, the universe and all that is. We return all that we have borrowed for the season of our own lifetime, as we return to our source.

46

Life With and Without Magic

Sometimes the magic works, sometimes it doesn't.[1]

A disputed but often repeated observation by Einstein is that one may either live as if there are no miracles or as if everything is. The intent of that observation, and probably of the real statements by Einstein connected to it, is that the universe is consistent and does what it does without external interference and exceptions. The implication is that anything the religious consider miracles, are either misunderstandings of natural occurrences or did not happen. My own experiences within the world of Christianity match the movie quote from *Little Big Man*. Sometimes the calls for magic help from outside of natural events appear to work, and most times they do not. Still, Old Lodge Skins and the Christians of my past continue to believe that the magic is real and available even if our experience tells us that it is unpredictable at best.

I see two major reasons for our belief in magic answers. One of them is protection and the other one is observation of things beyond our knowledge. Many sources on anthropology and religion are available which explore man's desire for protection from the adverse effects of unpredictable nature. If one believes that throwing a human victim or two into the caldera will prevent the volcano from melting the village, in they go! If one believes

---

1 *Little Big Man*, spoken by the character Old Lodge Skins, played by Dustin Hoffman.

that praying and the laying on of hands will protect the missionary from the risks of travel and the animosity of those who do not wish a new belief system, then on go the hands and up go the prayers. Despite all the times when nature still acts like nature and when bad things happen to people who were supposed to be protected, humans cling to practices which give them hope for power over what they fear.

The second reason is observing things which exceed our knowledge of the universe. I have personal experience of growing dizzy in Africa as a killer tornado passed close to my home and four daughters in Indiana. I have experienced physical renewal after prayers with no medical assistance. The December 2016 issue of *National Geographic* begins with a cover story on how beliefs do produce changes in physical outcomes. If one takes these events and generalizes them, religious teachings appear to be confirmed. If religious teachings become impossible to believe, I was raised to believe one is left with no explanation except coincidence. However, many of the events feel too powerfully connected for the mind and emotions to accept that there is no real connection. Other traditional examples come from natural events as mentioned above. If a mountain suddenly spews fire and death, then some God must be angry. It gives explanation to what at one time was unexplainable.

It now seems to me that we have more and more evidence that much of what seemed magic in the past can be understood within the normal rules of physics. What we recognize as matter and energy can emerge from a background which we consider to have been nothing. The behavior of small particles can be predicted in matched pairs across large distances with no known means of connection. The human body does heal itself in at least some cases based on belief in either religion, medical intervention, or both. I conclude that what we do in one place may in some cases effect what happens in another by natural means beyond our current explanations by physical capacities of the universe which do not require angel messengers or warriors. We are discovering things beyond our previous understandings that show connections beyond what simplistic explanations of the physical world told us were possible. Sometimes the magic works, and science is beginning to tell us why—within the physical laws of the universe.

I used to believe that this left us in a world without miracles. In the traditional sense, it does. It sounds much like the cosmos of the deists who believe the great watchmaker wound the universe and now sits back with no further interference. The practical person becomes much like Eustice as he first appears in *The Chronicles of Narnia*, by C. S. Lewis.[2] The only impressive things in the universe are our machines and the inventions man makes from the mundane elements of nature. I find that worldview very unsatisfying and it is not the territory my beliefs have entered.

I find myself in the universe where everything is miracle. Miracles from forces external to the universe are not needed because the cosmos itself produces all the awe and wonder the human mind can fathom. I do not have to believe that an angel or fairy is present to wonder at the simple opening of a flower, the passing of a storm, or the beauty of a hawk in flight. They are themselves, and they are all part of a universe so large and fantastic that the language of magic and miracle are often our best descriptions. I still tell people that I will pray for them and I keep the promise. I know that there is comfort in the connection of caring, and there is enough strangeness in the universe to allow room for the possibility that my positive energy here might indeed produce changes at a distance. Worship is still a reasonable descriptor for what I do in the forest, on a cliff, or when the trees on each side of the road have limbs that cross above creating a natural tunnel that sparks my Celtic imagination. Except it is the wonder of the time and place I am in plus my interaction with them that I celebrate in this worship. I do not have to believe in the supernatural to be amazed, awed and humbled by the natural world. I choose to live in a cosmos where everything is miracle.

---

2. Lewis, *Voyage of the Dawn Treader*.

47

Bosons and Discourse

One of the greatest scientific advancements of the new century is the confirmation of the Higgs boson and I have been working for some time to improve my understanding of it as a non-physicist. Using the best analogy for it, I have gone through a couple of false starts at interpreting which part of the story is the Higgs and what it does. This morning I watched a Ted lecture of David Miller's prize-winning analogy,[1] and it encourages me to continue with recent reflections on our reality.

In this analogy, a room is filled with physicists evenly dispersed at a social gathering. Then either Higgs himself walks in the room attracting people who want to discuss ideas, or just a piece of information is passed to those at the door and gradually crosses the room as groups of people hear it and congregate for a moment to discuss. The first version with a person crossing the room originally caused me some missteps as I thought the famous person, and later the people attracted, were the bosons. This wonderful short video makes it clear that it is the concentrations of people gradually shifting across the crowd that collectively represent the Higgs boson. The scientific implications for our basic understanding of the universe and the existence of mass—everything that we consider matter—are amazing. However, today I am contemplating the application of the analogy rather than the actual science.

In the analogy people are evenly spread around the room and nobody stands out as significant in the common background. But as an idea

---

1. Lincoln, "Higgs Field, Explained."

and the opportunity to discuss it passes through the crowd, small groups form into temporary clusters of greater density and have mass. Then they disperse again as the discussion moves on to the next group encountering the information. I believe it says some wonderful things for sociology, not just physics.

At the beginning, the people are unnamed and have no mass, no special significance. Then we add an idea, a concept, a mental or social construct so that interaction about it occurs bringing small collections together who now have mass; something significant is happening. When the idea passes along to the next group, each individual returns to random positions in the room and may again seem inconsequential.

To explain how I see this relating to real social phenomenon, and not just quantum physics, I need to note one thing I wish was obvious about people. While they all represent a common background, the Higgs field in the scientific analogy and a room full of physicists would not be the same in human reality. I pause for this because of those in the early twenty-first century who have come to see science and scientists as some unified conspiracy which opposes their particular religious views. The truth among academics is very obviously the opposite. Consensus does not come easily among the studies, competing theories, and egos of the academic world. A room full of physicists would contain a great variety of personalities, specific research foci, attitudes, and beliefs. Scattered to represent the background field in the analogy there is no commonality and no mass; or in common terms, weight, to their presence.

The background is formless, chaotic not in collisions of significance but in the unnoticed symmetry of pre-significance. The important event is an idea and the chance to discuss it entering the room! It is the energy of human thought and interaction that brings meaning into the illustration. As people interact and form social constructs we have the image of matter, substance, appearing.

This matches my current contemplations about our existence and significance. Alone, most of us are faceless pieces in an unimaginably large population. We work to determine and reassure ourselves of our individual significance, but often feel as inconsequential as a single bubble amid the deluge falling across Niagara. Alone, or talking with only those we happen to be in proximity to by ideology or geography, there is potential but something vital to being truly human is missing. There is little or no gravity in the moment.

Then we introduce an opportunity to gather to think and discuss an idea. And the image becomes exciting. Something of value begins to move across our experience. People with different views cluster to hear, debate, and form new constructs about some topic and something important comes into existence, something that exceeds our individual significance. Alone we represent potential; in groups, we take on mass and the potential to be building blocks of reality.

In the early years of this century, society seems to have become chaotic. We have become separated from each other. Much of the individual conversations at our cocktail party seem to indicate we have already consumed too much and have descended into talk with no more significance than a playground name calling contest. Nonetheless, I have recently observed people who came together because of some common idea—the remembrance of a valued colleague and her life's work, a celebration of the year's darkest physical day and the working of the solar system which will now begin increasing the light, a cluster of teachers reaffirming the significance of their work in the face of a disrespectful period of leadership—and something real happens.

People gathered around a topic become more than the sum of the individual parts. The situation gains significance and there is potential for the creation of larger things if only for a passing time. Sometimes the momentary existence of something bigger is all there is and it is enough. Sometimes whole new worlds emerge. I am now actively working for opportunities to be a catalyst for these moments. It is time to bring people, individuals who may be very different from each other, together for discourse. None of us knows what reality may manifest itself through unifying fields of thought in our time!

48

The Infinity Problem

There are many problems still facing those working toward a scientific theory of everything. While trying to determine the relationship of various forces and fields, new information comes to light which challenges our understanding of the individual elements science seeks to unify. Much of the theoretical work is done through complex mathematics. The formulas which appear to describe various behaviors of matter and energy, from the simple elegance of $E = mc2$ to equations that fill entire pages, are examined for possible combinations which could show how the various forces are related, or unified. The problem which arises when working with the equations of quantum and macro physics is that the result of the combined equations is an infinite answer.

Equations resulting in infinite answers are a problem for scientists and mathematicians. Infinity refuses to be further manipulated. Infinity cannot be added, subtracted, multiplied or divided. So, further work with the same set of equations becomes mathematically impossible. This prohibits the work of science to manipulate the ideas represented by the symbols in ways that lead to further understanding. The math has escaped into a realm beyond human understanding or manipulation. The effort to present an equation relating all fields or forces is brought to a standstill when the equations escape into answers of infinity. No theory can be expounded from them to be communicated with other scientists and certainly not to broader audiences. No manipulations of the forces can be designed to test theory or to create applications from the mathematical result.

The Infinity Problem

This problem looks very different through the lens of theology. Scientists often use phrases such as *finding God* as the goal of their efforts, although with a very different meaning than most theologians would except. They seek the bottom line understandings of existence. The unified theory should explain our origins, existence, and future. Set within that context, arriving at an answer of infinity seems quite logical from a background of theology which has always claimed that God is infinite. If one is looking for God and finds the infinite, the theological response might easily be, "Of course!"

While some of the top theorists have now suggested that there may never be a successful theory of everything, no single equation that contains all things in a way we can understand and manipulate, I have confidence that progress toward it will continue. Although the work already in progress exceeds my mathematical understanding, I still see and appreciate the brilliance of the minds at work. I watch developments from the various approaches and theories which appear with amazing regularity, often requiring reexamination of problems that were supposedly solved in the past. I expect constant discovery and change from the minds at work in both quantum and macro physics.

But, the current answer makes sense to me, even though my mind cannot comprehend or manipulate infinity better than anyone else's. If the current theories of worm holes and multiple universes are possibly true then an answer of infinite possibility seems highly logical with no mention of theology. When one uses the frameworks of theology, attempts to find and express the underlying cause and power behind all things resulting in an answer of infinity is also expected rather than problematic. A search for God that results in an answer of the infinite matches teachings which have existed for millennia.

Those who remain within the circle of faith in a deity separate from the physical world may find comfort and affirmation in these results. I find comfort in shifting to a realization that no search for an infinite beyond the observable world is required. The more we learn about the mysteries of the universe, the more we find that the universe itself contains the attributes we previously defined as God, the more fertile the unified field becomes for exploring theology.

49

Centering

Only he who has an impenetrable center in himself is free.[1]

One of the advantages of maintaining an established set of religious beliefs is a degree of certainty about knowing the center of truth and existence. If we accept the existence of an all-powerful God as the creator and sustainer of everything, then that God is surely the central character of all efforts to understand all else that is. What does twenty-first-century science say to us about this center if we hold our religious beliefs loosely?

Several years ago my friend Tim Van Meter and I dedicated our efforts in reading and exploring meaning to writings on meditation and contemplation. It was a valuable time for shifting our focus away from bondage to doctrine or dogma and into the world of experiencing God instead. Thelma Hall's book on the Catholic practice of *Lectio Divina*[2] was particularly helpful in moving from reading Scripture to know information about God or to clarify doctrine to instead reading in order to experience the Divine. Work in this type of practice often emphasizes going into our own center to find that place where God dwells within the human being. I found it very healthy and a way to be more open to experience of universal power rather than just discussing theologies. Then, after months of pursuing contemplation as

---

1. Tillich, *Eternal Now*, 17.
2. Hall, *Too Deep for Words*.

a new path, I discovered that I had become quite self-obsessed. Everything had become about my practice, my experience, and my feelings of being in the presence of the Divine. Missing was the focus on caring about others. My practice had become all about my own peace and well-being and very lacking in emphasis on looking outward toward my neighbors and the rest of the world which had always been central to my evangelical training. It did not feel right, and I changed toward a more balanced approach to life.³ Also turning his focus outward to the world, Tim went on to earn his PhD at Candler School of Theology and joined the faculty at Methodist Theological School in Ohio where his work maintains a major emphasis on ecology and sustainable human practices.⁴

As I worked to finish these essays, I also read *Convictions* by Marcus Borg. Near the end of the book, he speaks briefly about centering in God and includes the reference to Paul Tillich, quoted above. This quote of Tillich's has remained with me over the decades since I first saw it on a small slip of paper taped to the edge of a shelf in the office of my mentor. Tillich maintains that our very nature as individuals, and especially as thinking individuals, reveals to us that we are each alone—even when surrounded by others. As an alternative to loneliness, he suggests entering solitude where we can find each other in the divine center of all things. Considering the enriching possibility of those times when we reach into the center, he says, "In these moments of solitude something is done to us. The center of our being, the innermost self that is the ground of our aloneness, is elevated to the divine center and taken into it. Therein we can rest without losing ourselves."⁵ Here Tillich presents centering in the divine as the place where our aloneness can become community with others in the one place that includes every individual's center. I believe his words express a Christian path to seeing our place in the universe while we are alive rather than merely waiting for reunification when life ends.

This caused me to spend some days contemplating how a theology based on our approach to the unified field in science would compare to teachings and practices of meditation and contemplation. Can we find the center through unified field theology? Are we alone here on earth without

---

3. Readers wishing to study how attention to the inner life can include a healthy focus on the rest of the world as well may find great value in the writings of the American monk Thomas Merton.

4. Van Meter, *Created in Delight*.

5. Tillich, *Eternal Now*, 24.

a way to find the center unless we choose to believe certain religious teachings? Does the information now available to us through science open a way to approach these issues?

I believe it does. In 2016, Stephen Hawking created a television program where participants were given experiments and problems designed to help them see the universe as we are beginning to understand it. Experiments near the end of episode 4 dealt specifically with the issue of finding the center of the universe.[6] The experiments in this program led to consideration of the center of the universe by exploring conditions now and looking backward toward the moment of the big bang.

As we approach the moment of the big bang, we realize that everything that is draws closer and closer together. The spot in the cosmos which is us is drawn into greater and greater proximity to everything else that is. Eventually, everything is seen compressed into that one incredibly small point from which all matter and energy emerge. We are at the center where everything that will ever be emerges from that one tiny point. We are at the center and we are in unity with everything else that will ever be.

Looking in the other direction may seem more difficult. Everything continues to spread and separate. Perhaps now we have lost the center. As the universe expands we are here on our planet as everything continues to rush outward and away from us. And it may be difficult to see how that possibly connects us to the center. This is because we are used to watching explosions on earth bounded by our own time and location. If we picture a Hollywood special effects explosion, we see large amounts of debris flying in all directions and then falling to the ground. This leaves each piece in a separate location and most far from the center. Depending on the design put in place by the special effects team the resulting center may be easy to identify at the point where the explosives were detonated, or may be very difficult to find if the debris field was designed to expand in a direction other than an even circle. If we see our planet, as if it is one of those resulting shards, it appears obvious that we are anything but the center of the picture.

This is not an accurate view of the expanding cosmos. The big bang and the expansion of the universe do not occur in the restricted environment of our atmosphere or our planet's gravity. The expansion of the universe from the original point continues outward in uniform expansion. This is difficult for us to picture from our limited platform. Every part is moving away from

---

6. Hawking, "Where Did the Universe Come From?"

every other part in constantly expanding space-time. In this reality, each observational platform will show the rest of the universe expanding away from it in the same way as every other viewing platform. It is appropriate to say that every point is still the center with the universe moving constantly away, regardless of what point we use to make our observation.

I find that it makes an elegant model for consideration of human thought and centering activities. We can look backward toward the beginning and see ourselves at the center at the moment the universe springs into existence. Traveling to our ultimate origin, which we commonly refer to as the moment of creation, we are in the center of all things. We are united with all of the power and matter that will become all of the amazing features of the universe we are just beginning to view and understand. We find our common center with everything that is and the power that causes them to be. I believe this correlates very well with centering ourselves in God.

If we turn and look forward in time, we are still in the center but everything else has been spread far enough from us to view in wonder. Now we use our central observation point to look out and witness how large and diverse the world has become. We can appreciate it. We can feel the glory of being surrounded by it all. We can be humbled by the size and grandeur of the universe realizing that our center is now only one small spot. And we can rejoice in the beauty which is available to us from our tiny point of perspective.

This view of centering in the universe can also humble us. Every other point in the universe was also at the center when all things spread into being. Each place in the cosmos is still a center as the uniform expansion of space-time continues in every direction. We are blessed. We come from the same center as everything that is. We maintain our central viewing platform with opportunities to observe it all through very recent advancements in technology. What we do not find is permission to be puffed up and assume that we are of central importance and somehow above everything else. Every other point was also in the original center, remains its own center, and invites us to experience our oneness with it all without the hubris of claiming that we are the only center of meaning or purpose.

50

Reexamining Familiar Texts

I am now ready to revisit the religious texts of my youth, along with writings from other traditions allowing them to simply be. Any readers still within the conservative evangelical community have probably already abandoned all hope for these essays. Some believers from mainstream Christianity—people my childhood church called liberals and doubted whether they knew God—may find the place where I am now very familiar. I am ready to revisit poetry in the Bible and allow it to be poetry, stories and allow them to be stories, wisdom writings and allow them to be wisdom of an ancient culture and time. There is much in the collected wisdom literature of the world that can lead to clusters of meaningful discourse if we create open space to consider other views and see what new understandings emerge from the process.

If I do not demand these texts communicate the literal word of God to me, I can revisit them for the beauty of the expressions themselves. I can read them and consider what characteristics of these documents caused them to be valued, taught, and protected across millennia of human experience. I can consider which parts speak to me in ways that enrich life and which are part of a culture I would never approve. I no longer need to construct convoluted paths of hypocrisy to justify disobeying ancient commands to kill witches, defiant children, or prophets whose prophecies do not happen. I can affirm the beauty of traditions of charity for both the neighbor and the stranger without requiring everything from ancient culture to be of value in the twenty-first century.

Having let these traditional writings out of the box requiring everything to be true or false for all people and all times, I can read with the same joy that I read other sources. I can question the text without fear of defying a judgmental God. I can learn from scholars within the religion that produced the texts and not worry that I have abandoned the only true reading as taught by my local church. In short, I have a new life giving adventure available as I travel the pages of ancient literature and see what communicates something meaningful of truth or beauty without insisting that is the only truth.

I am free and I am ready.

51

The Two Trees of Genesis 2:9

Christians, especially the evangelicals and fundamentalists of my youth, look to this ancient text as the literal history of how mankind became separated from God, guilty before God by the simple act of birth into failed humanity, and in need of a sacrificial savior. I have discussed some of my concerns with this theology in earlier essays, the most serious being that it leaves the majority of earth's inhabitants living and dying as unforgiven members of rebel humanity doomed to eternal punishment with no access to any knowledge of the acts of God and the path of faith as outlined in the Bible. My purpose here is to contemplate a very different interpretation. After an embarrassing amount of my life listening to only Christian voices explaining ancient Jewish texts, I finally began reading Jewish scholars. There I encountered very different views that helped me to see life enriching applications of what seemed to be familiar texts.

One of these is the story of Adam and Eve in the garden of Eden allowed to eat of every good thing but warned not to choose the Tree of Knowledge of Good and Evil. In the interpretation I was raised to believe, this is presented as an actual happening in time; the wrong choice occurred once and exists for all time condemning humanity; and only salvation through Jesus Christ solves the problem created. I now love a very different interpretation. In rabbinic teaching, I encountered the idea, paralleled in Christian contemplative writings, to read the texts in the present and allow oneself to inhabit the narrative. Doing this with Genesis allows this ancient wisdom story to apply directly to life in any time.

The Two Trees of Genesis 2:9

Before us are two trees, two choices. One is life. The other is to separate ourselves from our humanity and life, to be gods, to be separate from and superior to nature and others. This choice leads to suffering and death. Instead of a one-time choice made for us all in the unrecoverable past, we can look at the choice as always existing. In each moment, we make choices of thought and action. Considered against the backdrop of this story of human origins, we can evaluate each choice based on whether we choose life or death. Taken literally, we seldom make such choices and hope we never have to do so. But, each thing we do, especially in interactions with others is still a choice to act in ways that separate us and lead to lessening of life or to act in ways that enrich our existence.

As I sit alone in my room reading social media posts, I encounter those which make me laugh or think positive thoughts and those which disturb and anger me. Then I choose my response. Liking those that please me is easy. The choices are clearer as I confront the ones that offend me. If I choose to let them pass or hide them, I am making an easy choice for life. If I respond with an angry response or just share them for others to see their negativity, I am choosing suffering. Occasionally, it is more complicated as when a post is offensive and harmful to other readers. Choosing life in these cases becomes more complex. Do I try to post a response of support for those under attack knowing this will also make the negative post show on my timeline? Perhaps I send a direct message to an individual or group of people letting them know they are loved and respected, but this does not publicly confront the abuse. I must consider each one for context and likely effects, but I can be guided by contemplating whether my action will support and improve life or add to suffering. If my response is designed to elevate myself and make myself appear better than others, it will likely be a choosing of death regardless of how craftily I word it.

When I am stuck in a slow line, I can contemplate my own response and whether I am choosing life or death. First, I do it for myself. I become aware of whether I am choosing to become restless and angry over a situation I cannot control. I can choose instead to turn on music which lifts my spirit; I can send a friendly message to my wife or a friend, or simply ask about their day and focus on their needs or joys; I can open one of the many resources I have with me and study or read for pleasure as technology now allows me to carry the world's libraries in my pocket! This way of thinking becomes especially meaningful to me when I reach the person trying to provide service at the front of the line. How will I interact with the cashier, the person at the drive-up window, or whose car has broken creating a traffic problem? I can express my displeasure at being inconvenienced by the slow line and let them know I consider myself too important to be bothered by their situation. This will add to their bad day, be a choice of death for them, and almost never leave me feeling any better. Or, I can choose to be pleasant, choose life. Over and over I have watched the face of a hardworking person in the midst of a difficult day change from expressions of stress, pain and/or anger to a wonderful smile of gratitude by simply smiling and interacting with them in a positive way. Choosing life, their day is brightened for at least a moment and my own is lifted as well.

The situations are as infinite as the interactions we experience. And in each one we can become aware of our own ability to stand before Eden's trees and selfishly choose death or make life better by choosing to taste of life. This alone has more meaning for me than the view on which I was raised. But, there is another beautiful layer to the interpretation. Each moment comes and passes in an instant whether I choose correctly or not. And I am in a new moment. The traditional evangelical reading of this text makes failure permanent, damaging both humankind and the planet itself pending some future divine rescue. This alternative read does not. If I realize I have chosen wrongly, I am back before the two trees. Is it a situation I can and should take time to go back and correct? This choice is before me. If it is a situation where the opportunity has come and passed, I can take stock and realize I can act in a different way in the future. And the future is always there immediately in front of us and confronting us with the same choice. Moving ahead into the day's next interaction, activity, or interruption, we get to choose again if we will listen to the ancient advice of Moses as the people prepared to enter a new land, "Choose life."[1]

---

1. Deuteronomy 30:19.

52

Humans and Nature in the Bible

Although I have seen people use the Bible to defend every kind of destruction, I want to revisit the texts for what they might say about humanity as part of nature. This is what science tells me we are, one part of a wonderful natural whole. So, it is interesting to look back at the old stories knowing who and what we are.

Genesis chapter 1 tells the story of all nature coming into being before humans making all the rest of nature our elders in the scheme of life. It can also set the context of humanity's need for the rest of nature in order to exist. Before there are humans, there is light and water, tree and flower, bird and beast. Then we arrive at home in the paradise of their companionship.

Genesis chapter 2 completes the story but reverses one key aspect. The creation of humans is placed first, as caretakers for the plants of the earth. Then all the animals enter the narrative and are brought to the human to identify and name. This second story, a real problem for those who insist that every verse is literally true, is an affirmation of the first if allowed to simply be itself. Humans and the rest of life are in a symbiotic relationship. We survive in the company of each other. Told from the view which most closely resembles the theories of science, we come late in the story as a final form of life to join the rest. Told this second way, the emphasis is on our need to live in a healthy way with the rest of life—a responsibility to use our abilities to think, reflect and plan to make sure that our relationship with nature is positive. Clearly the original owners of these texts saw no conflict, because the text has come down through the millennia with both versions included.

Then in chapter 3 a problem is quickly introduced. Here is the story so often labeled the *fall* in narratives that present humans as rebellious against God and in need of redemption. It is difficult to explain how two beings absent all knowledge of good and evil can bring judgment on themselves and all mankind for making the wrong decision. It makes sense as an ancient explanation of both how humans came to possess thinking skills which have been considered absent in other animals until recent times and as a Pandora's box accounting for why bad things happen. In the context of the first two chapters of Genesis, I see it making sense in another way. The attempt to do something new by eating the fruit was to become something more than the other animals, to be like God. Humans attempt immediately to see themselves as, or to actually be, something different and above the rest of nature. The power behind all things appears and the story shows them hiding because they already realize they are just naked animals. So, Creator helps them understand their role in the world and explains to them both what will be good and what will be hard in life on this planet. The fall? Perhaps it is no more than the fall from imagined separation and grandeur back to our place among the rest of nature.

By chapter 6 we encounter the strange story of Noah and the flood. Taken literally, it presents more problems than it answers despite the proclamations of those who recently built a life-size replica near my home in an attempt to show people how logical the story is. For one thing, God fails in the story as a literal history. God attempts to rid the world of evil by giving it a giant bath, and it does not work. This hardly fits the theological descriptions of God held by those who also defend the literalist view. Perhaps it fits the narrative considered here. Seen alongside other creation stories from around the world, it may be no more than a third telling of how both humanity and animals came to live on the planet. Or, it may be an explanation of a time of great flooding and survival. In either case, what interests me in thinking about humans and nature is that in order for life to continue, both humans and every kind of animal need to live. While some of us may scoff at the idea of the total fauna of the planet on one boat, perhaps if we let story be story it reminds us again of our unity with all the rest of life and that we are permanently, *all in the same boat*.

After the flood, we find humans again flourishing and reproducing in numbers sufficient to include various nations. This same strange appearance of many people happens in the origin stories where a man and a woman with two sons suddenly inhabit a world where the one who commits murder is worried about other people who will kill him as he travels. As story, this is not so much of a problem as time can pass in strange ways in fiction as long as the central theme is clear.

Then, in chapter 11 the story turns to the hubris of the people of Babel who decide and apparently have the ability in the narrative to build a tower to the heavens. The narrative lacks a clear explanation of why this would be a problem, except that God does not approve and does not want humans to be able to do everything their minds can imagine. So, the people are divided by languages and disperse across the earth. My favorite explanation of this in traditional teaching is that creatures capable of worshipping the Creator are spread to all parts of the earthly creation. But, the story presents it as another attempt at superiority by humans thwarted by the power of the universe. So, I look at it in continuation of the earlier chapters. Once again, humans are trying to lift themselves above the natural order and ascend to a special level. And again, they fail; affirming that the place of humanity is on this planet among the rest of the life that inhabits this sphere of rock and water.

The point is made and the emphasis is clear that the life well lived is about how one acts in the here and now. The rewards and punishments are now. The Jewish texts remain ambivalent about whether there is any life beyond this life. Different approaches to theology based on those texts come to different answers as to whether this life is the entirety of human existence. We are here. We are part of this world. And what we do matters and has its results here.

Christianity emerges and the Bible is assembled containing not just a version of the Torah and other ancient literature of Israel but also the writings of the early church. These writings place more and more emphasis on people as part of an unearthly kingdom. Prophetic writings appear and are reluctantly included that are often interpreted to say this world will end and yet humanity, at least the chosen, will continue. Some have interpreted these texts to indicate that humans are not bound to the rest of nature. Some have gone so far as to read into the prophecies that as soon as this world is destroyed, humanity will be freed to live without pain and suffering.

Those prophecies reach their conclusion in Revelation chapter 21. Here, the one who comes to set all things right proclaims the creation of a new heaven and a new earth and establishes the home of the Creator among humans on earth. If we agree that these writings belong in any way with the original accounts from the Torah, a challengeable argument to be sure but one that Christians traditionally accept, it seems to me that they remain in parallel with the emphasis on human beings belonging to earth as found in the earlier writings. The heavens are still separate from earth. And even though the power of the universe is said to come and abide with humanity, the location given for that existence is on a new earth. Setting aside the problems of God succeeding with fire where water failed and the idea that the current planet can literally be destroyed and humanity can survive to live happily on its replacement, the affirmation continues that the place of humans is on earth. In this idealized future, we are still here. Realizing the power of the universe as also here, humanity finally lives at peace with each other and the rest of nature. What might the result be if we truly believed that power is now here?

Every walk I take in the forest, every swim in the waters of lakes, rivers or oceans, and every climb upon the face of a rock affirms to me that this is true. We are forever linked to our planet. When all is right, humans live happily and harmoniously with the rest of life, here, on earth.[1]

---

1. A wonderful full-length presentation of similar ideas can be found in Bass, *Grounded*.

53

Science and the Book of Job

One of the books of the Bible that intrigues me is the ancient poem of Job. Taken as a literal text, this poem raises some odd questions about how God behaves toward man. The scenes where Satan challenges God and is allowed to torment this righteous man are hard reading for a literalist who maintains the supremacy of God. Why would God have any just or loving reason to allow the evil one to rain disasters on a good and holy man?[1]

Taken as a wisdom poem, it contains a number of treasures. It provides a strong argument against any worldview that says those who suffer are the cause of their own pain. The suffering human is allowed to express anguish and even challenge God and still be considered holy and a friend of God. The poem also affirms a creation where the suffering one is granted his requests even though they do not sound religious or holy for God to come to him in his troubles. God shows up.

The poem forcefully asserts that God is God and man does not have the knowledge or wisdom to understand what God does, how, or why. But, God does show up and takes the side of the suffering person, declares him a friend, and restores his health, life, and fortune.[2]

---

1. Schaeffer, *Affliction*, contains the best explanation I have encountered within the evangelical paradigm.

2. In another example of how these texts belong to a patriarchal past, the fact that the loss and restoration of family and fortune also happens to the wife is given little notice.

Unified Field Theology

What I want to do in this essay is to consider the possible answers of modern science to the challenges given to Job. Then I will consider what thoughts we might draw from this poem and our current knowledge and situation.

- Science now looks into the universe and claims that we can answer when Earth formed, its dimensions, and what the universe looked like in its first moments.
- We know that gravity holds the sea in place and moves it in the tides.
- We have technology to make light when and where we desire. We can see and record the acts that people do at night.
- We have explored the springs on the floor of the ocean and are close to journeying to the bottom of its deepest trenches.
- We now know the background origin of all things including light.
- We have explored the clouds and know their cause and how they work to produce each kind of precipitation. We fly through hurricanes to take their measure. We know the factors for the production of ice and we can create them.
- We are studying the core realities of life and death.
- We have been to the depths where no light reaches.
- We know the entire planet, its shapes, processes and changes.
- We are learning more everyday about the formation and behavior of stars and galaxies.
- We are also studying things such as quasars and black holes unknown at the time the poem of Job was written.
- We have claimed dominion over the earth.
- We can produce rain and create lightening.
- We know the behavior patterns of the animals, how they live and how they communicate.
- We can hunt the prey of lions and provide food for wild animals.
- We have been where the rarest of animals give birth and raise their young and have studied, documented and filmed them.
- We took the wild lands, tamed and used the donkeys and now choose where they may live.

- Yes, we tamed the ox to make it plow for us.
- Even water buffalo—still strong and wild enough to charge a machine gun—are controlled by small children and made to work for them.
- We know the behavior, ways, and speed of the ostrich.
- We have controlled the horse and we have bred them into varieties for our purposes of work, transportation, or entertainment. We control them and tell them what to do and when.
- We have tamed raptors and taught them to hunt for us and return to our hands.

THOUGHTS FOR TWENTY-FIRST-CENTURY UNDERSTANDING

I find it interesting that twenty-first-century humans have answers for the knowledge questions raised by God in this poem. It would be stretching things too far to claim that we can control all of the natural processes involved, or that we created the world. Still, our knowledge has grown beyond all limits the poet attributes to us. We know how things behave, including the universe back to the earliest seconds. We have taken control of the wild things and wild places and used them for our purposes, often in destructive ways. And my mind returns to the two trees of the garden.

In the story recorded in Genesis, humans chose knowledge over life. Reflection on this poem demonstrates how we have continued to grow in knowledge of many things, things once considered to be in the realm of God alone. We know a lot. We have information stored on our technology systems in such quantity that no human beings alive today will have time to view and analyze it all. I see us continuing to pursue the knowledge of all things.

But, the evidence does not suggest that we have grown equally in choosing life. The Christian literalist may answer that the garden was sealed and we do not have access to the Tree of Life. That is not where the text ends. God is said to have told the people of Israel through Moses to choose life. Christians believe in Jesus and salvation, a return to life, purchased on the *tree* of the cross. He is quoted as teaching his followers that he was the "Way, the Truth, and the Life."[3] I believe that examining the entirety of the

---

3. John 14:6.

biblical texts indicates that humanity has been given access to the option of choosing life as well as knowledge.

And yet our leaders, often with support from the communities of faith, choose to use our knowledge of earth in ways that give us current rewards but also bring death to others now and in the future. We deplete the resources of the earth and use them in ways which change the environment in deadly ways. When resources are scarce in one place, we take up arms and make war on other members of humanity in order to maintain our habits of consumption and entertainment. Having learned so much, we miss the central point of the challenge. We are not gods. We do not possess the power to understand or to control all things. We may not have the power to undo the damage we are doing to our own planet.

With all we have learned, I believe it is time to stand before the two trees of Eden and decide if we are capable of collectively choosing life. This is a central hope for what I am proposing as unified field theology.

54

Our Most Powerful Myth

> John 1:1 In the beginning was the Word, and the Word was with God, and the Word was God. 2 He was with God in the beginning. 3 Through him all things were made; without him nothing was made that has been made. 4 In him was life, and that life was the light of all mankind. 5 The light shines in the darkness, and the darkness has not overcome it.

If you are offended by an essay titled myth beginning with this text, I am amazed you are still with me in pursuing these thoughts and contemplations. I salute you for your endurance! However, I am not recording these thoughts for those who are sure their beliefs are facts. If you are sure everything you have studied and been taught is factually true, I invite you to consider the contemplations of how your life embodies those teachings, and hope your faithfulness to your tradition empowers you to live in a way that enhances life for both yourself and "the least of these."[1]

I am writing for those like myself who find ourselves unable to be sure we know the one true explanation of all life, unable to accept a God who excludes most of humanity from that knowledge or the salvation that accompanies it, and seeking a new way to encounter both the universe and our traditions. So, I will consider this story of Jesus as a myth with a brief

---

1. Matthew 25:40.

reminder that I do not equate myth with lie but as the stories which contain our greatest hopes. Story and myth give voice to our attempts to explain truth which transcends simple statements of fact. This is for me, now as in my past, the most beautiful of all stories—if not overloaded with the dogma and judgment of others.

The force which brings the universe into existence is described as the Word. This echoes the ancient traditions which say God spoke and the universe is. In China, I encountered Tao as an expression of that Word without attachment to anything in man's observed world. I can easily pair it with that moment in physics when what appears to be nothing suddenly expresses itself in quanta appearing as pure energy and then forming into combinations we call the physical world. A power beyond even today's most complex explanations forms a universe so large we are only beginning to understand its size or the mysteries of its composition. That moment, that "Let there be,"[2] that power encompasses what we have been taught to label God, a term which is actually a simplification of many ancient words even among the traditions which believe in only one Creator.

So, the universe comes into being in all its amazing size, diversity, complexity and beauty. And on our small planet, humans arrive to live, wonder, laugh, love, suffer and die. Much of life is good. We are exactly suited for the planet we live upon and our pleasures are beyond counting. But, so are our troubles. From earliest times, we have exhibited the disturbing trait of killing each other, as well as other forms of life beyond any need for our own survival. Our bodies coexist with microorganisms which sometimes are helpful to us and sometimes cause our bodies to feel pain and to die. The amazing cycle of water and wind which recycles the planet's basic resource and sustains life sometimes produces storms that can kill us even after doing our best to find and build shelter. Accidents happen and life departs the body suddenly and without warning. And we feel pain. We not only feel physical pain, we suffer from minds which can question existence and loss. We possess the ability to suffer from our lack of understanding. While many of us were raised on a particular theology that said we suffer because the original man and woman chose to partake of the fruit of knowing what God knows, we suffer from the realization that we do not know what makes it all work. We do not know why in one instance nature's forces work and life is sustained and in another its workings cause life to cease.

2. Genesis 1.

For me, this is the great beauty of the story of Jesus of Nazareth. That universal power, able to bring forth worlds beyond worlds, able to give and sustain life, which is the source and destination of all things, notices us. The power beyond all our ability to understand includes knowledge of our pain and suffering. And it chooses to take the form of one of us. The power of the universe which would continue just the same whether our species, planet or solar system ceased to exist, notices us in our confusion and pain and chooses to invade our darkness as one of us.

Is this not the heart of many of our great stories? The gods look down on human life and choose to intervene in some way to alleviate suffering. A god chooses to give up life among the immortals because of the love of a human being. The royal chooses to leave the luxury of the castle to live a life of love with a common member of the kingdom. There are many varieties of this theme of power choosing to come from the safety of life beyond our suffering to love at least one of us.

In the story of Jesus of Nazareth, the universal power chooses to take on mortality to be with us. The power which transcends our comprehension chooses to share our powerlessness and suffering, to experience life as we experience it, and to share with us light—knowledge of what it all means. This is not an idea which is unique to Christianity. The ancient Jewish texts also speak often of the God who lives among men and interacts with them. Looking into the vastness of eternity or even the universe of this moment we are overwhelmed. Here is the beauty of a story that dares to say the power of that universe is willing to join us as we walk through life on this watery rock.

And the story of Jesus goes further. Having lived the life of a human and having experienced the frailty of our existence, wept for the loss of friends, and taught us that we are to care for one another as the most basic of human acts, Jesus goes a step further. The power behind and in all things chooses to die, not simply to be for a time and then depart. The force behind all life chooses to suffer death in one of its most horrible forms with arms outstretched to absorb our suffering and isolation. The story of sweating drops of blood on the Mount of Olives tells us the choice is made with no blindness to the depth that pain will take. My favorite sentence in the whole story is when Jesus on the cross cries out, "Eloi, Eloi, lama sabachthani?"[3] Here is the cry of humanity. Here is our small lost cry of pain in the face of a vast universe with no hint of connection to magic external power to fix

---

3. Mark 15:34.

it all. Here is the cry of abandonment and hopelessness. This is the trading of the immortal for the mortal, the existential cry of pain in a universe too vast to understand or control. Here is the claim that the very power we can never fully comprehend, fully understands us and loves us.

Then the story of Jesus proceeds to resurrection, "The light shines in the darkness, and the darkness has not overcome it."[4] If this was only the great escape, the story would fail. Instead it tells us that the power of the universe is greater than our greatest pain and fears. That which creates, sustains, and receives all things absorbs our worst suffering and still shines in the darkness. There is hope beyond our darkest nights.

It is a beautiful story. The power of everything knows and loves us, becomes us, suffers with us, and reassures us that life continues. I would still love this story if only for its archetypal beauty and power. It is comforting. And, it is inspiring. Believed as an actual account of how God behaves it sets the example which heroic figures follow. As great myth, it can still serve to inform life and our treatment of others. Recognizing the beauty of the story can inspire us toward the beauty of living in the same way. When we witness suffering from the crying of one small child to the city or country devastated by natural event or war, it invites us to act in ways that absorb the suffering. We can leave our comfort for the moment to help the child back home with their broken bicycle, to feed the hungry, clothe the naked, and free the prisoner.[5] When we recognize our own need for the comfort of one who chooses to act, we act.

And here is a point of contact between the individual who no longer believes the theology of their youth and the family which still sees that theology as the Truth. Here is a way home to fellowship with those who fear for our eternal destiny. We can choose not to argue about what is factually true or the failures of theology with those who are unprepared for those discussions and who still find comfort within their traditions. We can focus on how this beautiful account of sacrificial living invites us to live in the world. We can find common ground in our beliefs about the human life fully lived.

---

4. John 1:5.
5. Matthew 25.

55

New Fundamentals

> He has shown you, O mortal, what is good. And what does the Lord require of you? To act justly and to love mercy and to walk humbly with your God. —Micah 6:8
>
> Jesus replied: "'Love the Lord your God with all your heart and with all your soul and with all your mind.' 38 This is the first and greatest commandment. 39 And the second is like it: 'Love your neighbor as yourself.' 40 All the Law and the Prophets hang on these two commandments." —Matthew 22:37-39
>
> And now these three remain: faith, hope and love. But the greatest of these is love. —1 Corinthians 13:13

As I have worked through the teachings of my church tradition, the knowledge of the universe revealed by science, and the effects of chosen beliefs on human behavior, I have often contemplated what remains. Much of what I was taught was fundamental—baseline, required, and nonnegotiable—has fallen away as culturally restricted, internally inconsistent, or harmful to others in practice. And I am left to consider what remains. The ability of wealth and power to exert their privilege over those with less continues to be evident across many parts of human culture. But, there is little about it that I can accept as personal practice or teaching to share with others. There must be something superior which leads to lives that are fully human.

Unified Field Theology

When I look back to my own traditions, I find hope in these three passages from an ancient prophet, Jesus of Nazareth, and Paul, the founder of Christianity as a religion. First, they have obvious parallels. Humans are to walk in humility recognizing that we are very small compared to the size and power inherent in the universe. We can look out into the vastness with fear and doubt, or with awe and wonder. All three of these passages call humans to respond with love for the world and the power that sustains it and us. Further we are to live in hope that we can find a proper place in the world by practicing justice and mercy toward others, by loving humanity beyond our own group. The conclusion found in Jesus' answer and Paul's summary is that beyond all else what remains is love. Justice and mercy recommended by the ancient prophet are behaviors which show love rather than merely contemplating, discussing, or creating theories about it.

What strikes me about this way of seeing is that it does not require lengthy or complicated theologies, catechisms, or statements of faith. None of these three passages says anything about memorizing, affirming, or requiring others to accept any specific set of beliefs. Everything in them is about affect and action, not proprietary dogmas. There is nothing in them about any *us* being superior to a different *them*. We are all part of us. We share our place on this small but beautiful rock supplied with all we need to live. And we have mental capacity to examine life writ both large and specific and consider what it means to be human and live a positive life. And here we have guidance that is hard to deny. What is there to object to if a person treats others and the earth with justice, applies mercy when they perceive that they are wronged, and walks through life in humble awareness of how small and mortal we are?

I like these fundamentals because they do not exclude others. I have quoted them from the Bible, but they are also found in native teachings and ancient wisdom literature from around the world. There is nothing in them that contradicts what I have heard from the Dalai Lama, learned from Native friends, or read in the teachings of the rabbis. This universality answers one of the problems with the religious script I learned from childhood. The populations on what we now call North and South America did not have to hear of the ancient patriarchs or the life and death of Jesus to arrive at the same conclusions about life well lived. Neither are the ancients of the Far East or sub-Saharan Africa excluded. The correctness of such a life has been affirmed across cultures and vast periods of time without restriction to only one group chosen to have life while the rest of the world perishes in ignorance.

Using these guidelines for a proper life also refuses to be distracted by the fate of humans in an unknowable eternity. I am exploring this aspect of Jewish teachings. From my background in Christianity, it would seem that a people subjected more than once to hundreds of years of foreign captivity, the Roman diaspora, and the holocaust of the twentieth century might have found comfort in promises of a blissful life beyond the one we know. Yet, while there are Jewish beliefs about the soul as eternal, the focus has remained on life here and our choices of how to live—an emphasis on what we know and have control over instead of unknowns and wishful promises. What happens to our essence when the body expires will take care of itself no matter what we believe. What life is like in the present is under our control and we can choose how to treat each other in each new moment and interaction.

We know *heaven* and *hell* in the present tense. We can easily identify situations where those affected by disaster, disease, or war are living in the misery that common language easily calls hell. We rejoice together when life events, the opportunity to witness natural wonder, or the kindness of strangers brings us into situations of joy. We treasure mystic encounters that lift us into momentary experience of heaven. Living out love by making sure our own actions are just and merciful toward others increases our faith in each other and in the goodness of life, brings hope even in the midst of tragedy, and demonstrates humility which recognizes the collective importance of life as superior to narrow self-interest. It excludes no one as less and elevates none as superior to others. We are each invited simply to live life in ways that bring heaven closer to us all.

Emancipation from rules and promises of achieving holy status for special rewards and avoiding eternal punishment in invisible worlds beyond our knowledge can also free us from keeping lifelong checklists of whether we are *in* or *out*. I know many Christians who would respond here that trust in Jesus alone yields the same result. And yet when anybody starts living in ways they do not approve, I hear the doubts expressed about whether the person was really saved at all. People start becoming alarmed about the person's place in eternity, as some will do for me if they read these essays. Stepping aside from all of that, I believe is healthy. Whatever eternity is, is. If I quit trying to make sure I have earned my golden ticket, I can focus on each new moment. I have also seen much of this wisdom in

Jewish teachings. If I realize that I have acted in an unloving way, or failed to show mercy, I do not need to quake before an angry God. I can humbly turn to the next moment and choose how I will act in the next situation and what amends I may make to anyone I have offended. In fact, justice, mercy, humility and love invite us to stop focusing primarily on ourselves at all. They invite us to look outward to see where justice is needed, where mercy can be given, and where love can be demonstrated in real acts of caring. Perhaps we can finally live lives that demonstrate that we love our neighbors as ourselves.

This is where I am now. I choose to affirm that the universe is majestic and beyond me and am grateful for all that it provides to make life possible and enjoyable on earth. I choose to examine my decisions and actions for whether I am treating others fairly with the scales tilted in favor of mercy toward my brother or sister when I feel wronged. I choose to admit how small I am on our planet flying through a universe beyond my comprehension, and I choose love. We do not have to look the same, live the same, or agree on much of anything in order to recognize each other as fellow travelers through a life we only begin to understand. And we can desire the best for each other working to make sure our own acts promote the best possible circumstances each time we interact.

I am not God to require it of anyone else. But, I become more fully human as I require it of myself, and I invite you to contemplate the power that this unified field theology might provide for your own well-being and sense of belonging in the world that is.

Bibliography

Adar, Ruth. "Where Do You Sacrifice the Animals?" *Coffee Shop Rabbi* (blog). February 23, 2015. https://coffeeshoprabbi.com/2015/02/23/sacrifices/.
Bass, Diana. *Grounded: Finding God in the World: A Spiritual Revolution*. San Francisco: HarperOne, 2015.
Bell, Rob. *Love Wins: A Book about Heaven, Hell, and the Fate of Every Person Who Ever Lived*. New York: HarperCollins, 2011.
Borg, Marcus. *Convictions: How I Learned What Matters Most*. New York: HarperOne, 2014.
Brown, Gregory. "We Want to Learn and Succeed: Expelled Middle School Students Discuss School Community." Doctoral thesis, Indiana University, 1996.
Campbell, Joseph. *The Power of Myth*. New York: Anchor, 1991.
Carroll, Sean. *The Big Picture*. New York: Dutton, 2016.
Cash, Johnny. "The Far Side Banks of Jordan." August 2, 2005. Disc 2, track 17 on *Keep on the Sunny Side—June Carter Cash: Her Life in Music*. Columbia/Legacy.
Chan, Francis, and Preston Sprinkle. *Erasing Hell: What God Said about Eternity, and the Things We've Made Up*. Colorado Springs: Cook, 2011.
Cords, Nicholas, and Patrick Gerster. *Myth and the American Experience*. Beverly Hills: Glencoe, 1973.
Curry, Andrew. "Gobekli Tepe: The World's First Temple?" *Smithsonian* magazine, November 2008. http://www.smithsonianmag.com/history/gobekli-tepe-the-worlds-first-temple-83613665/.
Dylan, Bob. "Death Is Not the End." February 22, 2008. Track 4 on *Down in the Groove*. SBME Special.
Edwards, Jonathan. "Sinners in the Hands of an Angry God." Sermon preached at Enfield, July 8, 1741. Edited by Reiner Smolinski. Electronic Texts in American Studies. Paper 54. http://digitalcommons.unl.edu/etas/54.
Galeon, Dom, and Sarah Marquart. "The Universe Is Far Bigger Than We Thought, and It Has 10x More Galaxies." Futurism.com. October 14, 2016. https://futurism.com/the-universe-is-far-bigger-than-we-thought-and-it-has-10x-more-galaxies/.
Gold, Martin, and David Mann, eds. *Expelled to a Friendlier Place: A Study of Effective Alternative Schools*. Ann Arbor: University of Michigan Press, 1984.
Guthrie, Arlo. "Wake Up Dead." February 20, 1996. Track 7 on *Mystic Journey*. Rising Son Records.
Hall, Thelma. *Too Deep for Words: Rediscovering Lectio Divina*. New York: Paulist, 1988.

Bibliography

Hawking, Stephen. "Where Did the Universe Come From?" Script. *Genius*, season 1, episode 4. PBS, 2016. https://www.springfieldspringfield.co.uk/view_episode_scripts.php?tv-show=genius-by-stephen-hawking-2016&episode=s01e04.

Hebraic Literature: Translations from the Talmud, Midrashim and Kabbala. Translated and edited by Maurice Harris. New York: Tudor, 1943. Kindle Version, 2012.

Herzog, Harold. "Does Animal-Assisted Therapy Really Work?" *Psychology Today*, November 17, 2014. Available at the Animal Studies Repository. https://works.bepress.com/harold-herzog/69/.

Krauss, Lawrence. *A Universe from Nothing: Why There Is Something Rather Than Nothing.* Afterword by Richard Dawkins. New York: Free Press, 2013.

Kushner, Harold. *When Bad Things Happen to Good People.* New York: Avon, 1981.

Lemmel, Helen. "Turn Your Eyes upon Jesus." 1922. Public Domain. https://hymnary.org/text/o_soul_are_you_weary_and_troubled.

Lennon, John. "Imagine." Released September 9, 1971. Track 1 on *Imagine*. Apple Records.

Lewis, C. S. *The Chronicles of Narnia.* New York: HarperCollins, 1983.

———. *A Grief Observed.* New York: Bantam, 1976.

———. *The Voyage of the Dawn Treader.* New York: HarperCollins, 1983.

Lincoln, Don. "The Higgs Field, Explained." YouTube video, 3:18. Published by TED-Ed, August 27, 2013. https://www.youtube.com/watch?v=joTKd5j3mzk.

Lincoln, Yvonna, and Egon Guba. *Naturalistic Inquiry.* Beverly Hills: Sage, 1985.

Little Big Man. Film. 1970. Written by Thomas Berger (novel) and Calder Willingham (screenplay). Directed by Arthur Penn. Cinema Center Films and Stockbridge-Hiller Productions. Paramount Home Video, 2003.

Lockyer, Joshua, and James Veteto. *Environmental Anthropology Engaging Ecotopia: Bioregionalism, Permaculture, and Ecovillages.* New York: Berghahn, 2015.

Lopez, Barry. *Crow and Weasel.* New York: Square Fish, 1998.

Manning, Brennan. *The Ragamuffin Gospel: Good News for the Bedraggled, Beat-up, and Burnt Out.* Portland, OR: Multnomah, 1990.

Marley, Bob. "Get Up, Stand Up." Written by Bob Marley and Peter Tosh. Released October 1973. Disc 1, track 4 on *Bob Marley and the Wailers: Gold*. Kingston, Jamaica: Island Studios Tuff Gong Records.

McLuhan, Marshall, and Quinton Fiore. *The Medium Is the Massage: An Inventory of Effects.* New York: Bantam, 1967.

Mosher, Dave. "Elon Musk Has Published a New Study about His Ambitious Plans to Colonize Mars with SpaceX." *Business Insider*, March 27, 2018. https://www.businessinsider.com/elon-musk-mars-colony-details-new-space-study-2018-3.

Palmer, Parker. *The Courage to Teach: Exploring the Inner Landscape of a Teacher's Life.* San Francisco: Jossey-Bass, 1998.

———. *To Know as We Are Known: Education as Spiritual Journey.* San Francisco: HarperOne, 1992.

———. *The Promise of Paradox: A Celebration of Contradictions in the Christian Life.* San Francisco: Jossey-Bass, 2008.

Popper, Karl. *The Logic of Scientific Discovery.* London: Routledge, 2002.

Porter, Gene Stratton. *A Girl of the Limberlost.* Springfield Gardens, NY: Palmera, 2015.

Powell, Corey. "Is the Universe Conscious?" NBCNews.com. June 19, 2017. https://www.nbcnews.com/mach/science/universe-conscious-ncna772956.

Schaeffer Edith. *Affliction: A Compassionate Look at the Reality of Pain and Suffering.* Grand Rapids: Baker, 1993.

Bibliography

Schaeffer, Francis. *How Should We Then Live: The Rise and Decline of Western Thought and Culture*. Old Tappan, NJ: Revell, 1976.

Schaeffer, Francis, and C. Everett Koop. *Whatever Happened to the Human Race? Exposing Our Rapid Yet Subtle Loss of Human Rights*. Old Tappan, NJ: Revell, 1979.

Schwartz, Peter, and James Ogilvy. *The Emergent Paradigm: Changing Patterns of Thought and Belief*. Menlo Park, CA: SRI International, 1979.

Stewart, Tim. "God Said It, I Believe It, That Settles It." *Dictionary of Christianese*. July 29, 2013. http://www.dictionaryofchristianese.com/god-said-it-i-believe-it-that-settles-it/.

Tillich, Paul. *The Eternal Now*. New York: Scribner, 1963.

Van Meter, Timothy. *Created in Delight: Youth Ministry and the Mending of the World*. Eugene, OR: Wipf and Stock, 2013.

Zevon, Warren. "The Indifference of Heaven." Released April 13, 1993. Track 15 on *Learning to Flinch*. Nashville. Zevon Music, BMI.

www.ingramcontent.com/pod-product-compliance
Lightning Source LLC
Chambersburg PA
CBHW062043220426
43662CB00010B/1621